Former Female Slave
Narratives
&
Interviews:
From Ex-Slaves in the States of
Arkansas, Florida, Louisiana, Tennessee, Texas, and Virginia
With Photographs

By

Joe Mitchell, MA

Interviews conducted
By
Federal Writers' Project

HISTORIC PUBLISHING

San Antonio, Texas

PREPARED FOR PUBLICATION BY
HISTORIC PUBLISHING

Slavery Books & African American History Courses & Resources
https://africanamericanhistorybooks.blogspot.com

WWW.HISTORICPUBLISHING.COM

**PREPARED FOR PUBLICATION
BY
HISTORIC PUBLISHING**

CONTENTS

Introduction

American slave narratives are a unique and fascinating historical resource. Although, the narratives have their contextual limitations-they are an invaluable primary source that allows one to gain insight pertaining to slaves from their own perspective.

Former Female Slave Narratives is the product of the author's interest in the institution of slavery in all its facets. The narratives and interviews contained in this volume were selected based on a specific set of variables and criteria. It is the intent of the author to present narratives that documented slave life, folklore, the Civil War, and Emancipation. In addition, we include female slaves who were house slave, field workers, as well as those who were affiliated with Native Americans on some level. The subjects were chosen in an attempt to give the readers historical, ethnic, and social context of slavery in America. Moreover, we have chosen to include female narratives from a variety of states.

Another interesting facet of the narratives is that some of them actually include the former slave's residential address. It is a unique experience to see these places today. Obviously, the slave homes are most likely a casualty of time and progress. Nonetheless, some of the geographic locales still use the same addresses and street names, which allow those who are interested to note how the areas have changed over time.

Former Female Slave
Narratives
&
Interviews

Narratives in the Slave Narrative Collection by State

State	Narratives*
Alabama	129
Arkansas	677
Florida	67
Georgia	184
Indiana	62
Kansas	3
Kentucky	34
Maryland	22
Mississippi	26
Missouri	84
North Carolina	176
Ohio	32
Oklahoma	75
South Carolina	274
Tennessee	26
Texas	308
Virginia	15

* Number of narratives in collection may not match number in appendix as some narratives have been divided for improved searchability.

1. TEXAS SLAVE NARRATIVE
CLARISSA SCALES

Clarissa Scales, 79, was born a slave of William Vaughan, on his plantation at Plum Creek, Texas. Clarissa married when she was fifteen. She owns a small farm near Austin, but lives with her son, Arthur, at 1812 Cedar Ave., Austin.

"Mammy's name was Mary Vaughan and she was brung from Baton Rouge, what am over in Louisiana, by our master. He went and located on Plum Creek, down in Hays County.

"Mammy was a tall, heavy-set woman, more'n six foot tall. She was a maid-doctor after freedom. Dat mean she nussed women at childbirth. She allus told me de last thing she saw when she left Baton Rouge was her mammy standin' on a big, wood block to be sold for a slave. Dat de last time she ever saw her mammy. Mammy died 'bout fifty years ago. She was livin' on a farm on Big Walnut Creek, in Travis County. Daddy done die a year befo' and she jes' grieves herself to death. Daddy was sho' funny lookin', 'cause he wore long whiskers and what you calls a goatee. He was field worker on de Vaughan plantation.

"Master Vaughan was good and treated us all right. He was a great white man and didn't have no over seer. Missy's name was Margaret, and she was good, too.

"My job was tendin' fires and herdin' hawgs. I kep' fire goin' when de washin' bein' done. Dey had plenty wood, but used corn cobs for de fire. Dere a big hill corn cobs near de wash kettle. In de evenin' I had to bring in de hawgs. I had a li'l whoop I druv dem with, a eight-plaited rawhide whoop on de long stick. It a purty sight to see dem hawgs go under de slip-gap, what was a rail took down from de bottom de fence, so de hawgs could run under.

"Injuns used to pass our cabin in big bunches. One time dey give mammy some earrings, but when they's through eatin' they wants dem earrings back. Dat de way de Injuns done. After feedin' dem, mammy allus say, 'Be good and kind to everybody.'

"One day Master Vaughan come and say we's all free and could go and do what we wants. Daddy and mammy rents a place and I stays until I's fifteen. I wanted to be a teacher, but daddy kep' me hoein' cotton most de time. Dat's all he knowed. He allus told me it was 'nough larnin' could I jes' read and write. He never even had dat much. But he was de good farmer and good to me and mammy.

"Dere was a school after freedom. Old Man Tilden was de teacher. One time a bunch of men dey calls de Klu Klux come in de room and say, 'You git out of here and git 'way from dem niggers. Don' let us cotch you here when we comes back.' Old Man Tilden sho' was scart, but he say, 'You all come back tomorrow.' He finishes dat year and we never hears of him 'gain. Dat a log schoolhouse on Williamson Creek, five mile south of Austin.

Clarissa Scales

2. INTERVIEW OF MRS. FANNIE BERRY, EX-SLAVE 861 E. BANK STREET—PETERSBURG, VIRGINIA
BY SUSIE BYRD, PETERSBURG, VIRGINIA
DATE—FEBRUARY 26, 1937

NAT TURNER

Back 'fore the sixties, I can 'member my Mistress, Miss Sara Ann, comin' to de window an' hollerin', "De niggers is arisin'! De niggers is arisin'! De niggers is killin' all de white folks, killin' all de babies in de cradle!" It must have been Nat Turner's Insurrection; which wuz sometime 'fo de breakin' of de Civil War.

I wuz waitin' on table in dinin' room an' dis day dey had finished eatin' early an' I wuz cleanin' off table. Don't you know I must have been a good size gal.

JOHN BROWN

Yes, I 'member something 'bout him too. I know my Master came home an' said, dat on his way to de gallows ole John stopped an' kissed a little nigger child. "How com' I don't 'member? Don't tell me I don't 'cause I do. I don't care if its done bin a thousand years." I know what Master said an' it is as fresh in my mind as it wuz dat day. Dis is de song I herd my Master sing:

Old John Brown came to Harpers Ferry Town,

Purpose to raise an insurrection;

Old Governor Wise put the specks upon his eyes

An' showed him the happy land of Canaan.

INVENTION

My Master tole us dat de niggers started the railroad, an' dat a nigger lookin' at a boilin' coffee pot on a stove one day got the idea dat he could cause it to run by putting wheels on it. Dis nigger being a blacksmith put his thoughts into action by makin' wheels an' put coffee on it, an' by some kinder means he made it run an' the idea wuz stole from him an' dey built de steamengine.

RELATIONSHIP

I wuz one slave dat de poor white man had his match. See Miss Sue? Dese here ol' white men said, "what I can't do by fair means I'll do by foul." One tried to throw me, but he couldn't. We tusseled an' knocked over chairs an' when I got a grip I scratched his face all to pieces; an dar wuz no more bothering Fannie from him; but oh, honey, some slaves would be beat up so, when dey resisted, an' sometimes if you'll 'belled de overseer would kill yo'. Us Colored women had to go through a plenty, I tell you.

MARRIAGE

Elder Williams married me in Miss Delia Mann's (white) parlor on de crater road. The house still stands. The house wuz full of Colored people. Miss Sue Jones an' Miss Molley Clark (white), waited on me. Dey took de lamps an' we walked up to de preacher. One waiter joined my han' an' one my husband's han'. After marriage de white folks give me a 'ception; an', honey, talkin' 'bout a table—hit wuz stretched clean 'cross de dinin' room. We had everythin' to eat you could call for. No, didn't have no common eats. We could sing in dar, an' dance ol' squar' dance all us choosed, ha! ha! ha! Lord! Lord! I can see dem gals now on dat flo'; jes skippin' an' a trottin'. An' honey, dar wuz no white folks to set down an' eat 'fo yo'.

WAR

Now, Miss Sue, take up. I jes' like to talk to you, honey 'bout dem days ob slavery; 'cause you look like you wan'ta hear all 'bout 'em. All 'bout de ol' rebels; an' dem niggers who left wid de Yankees an' were sat free, but, poor things, dey had no place to go after dey got freed. Baby, all us wuz helpless an' ain't had nothin'.

I wuz free a long time 'fo' I knew it. My Mistess still hired me out, 'til one day in talkin' to de woman she hired me to, she, "God bless her soul", she told me, "Fannie yo' are free, an' I don't have to pay your Master for you now." You stay with me. She didn't give me no money, but let me stay there an' work for vitals an' clothes 'cause I ain't had no where to go. Jesus, Jesus, God help us! Um, Um, Um! You Chillun don't know. I didn't say nothin' when she wuz tellin' me, but done 'cided to leave her an' go back to the white folks dat fus own me.

I plan' to 'tend a big dance. Let me see, I think it wuz on a Thursday night. Some how it tooken got out, you know how gals will talk an' it got to ol' Bil Duffeys ears (ol' dog!) an', baby do you know, mind you 'twont slavery time, but de 'oman got so mad cause I runned away from her dat she get a whole passel of 'em out looking for me. Dar wuz a boy, who heard 'em talkin' an' sayin' dey wuz goin' to kill me if I were found. I will never forget dis boy com' up to me while I wuz dancin' wid another man an' sed, "nobody knowes where you ar', Miss Moore, dey is lookin' fer you, an' is gwine kill you, so yo' come on wid me." Have mercy, have mercy my Lord, honey, you kin jes 'magin' my feelin' fer a minute. I couldn't move. You know de gals an' boys all got 'round me an' told me to go wid Squreball, dat he would show me de way to my old Mistess house. Out we took, an' we ran one straight mile up de road, den through de woods, den we had to go through a straw field. Dat field seem' like three miles. After den, we met another skit of woods. Miss Sue, baby my eyes, (ha! ha! ha!) wuz bucked an' too if it is setch a thin' as being so scared yo' hair stand on yo' head, I know, mine did. An' dat wasn't all, dat boy an' me puffed an' sweated like bulls. Was feared to stop, cause we might have been tracked.

At last we neared de house an' I started throwin' rocks on de porch. Child I look an' heard dat white 'oman when she hit dat floor, bouncin' out dat bed she mus' felt dat I wuz comin' back to her. She called all de men an' had 'em throw a rope to me an' day drawed me up a piece to de window, den I held my arms up an' dey snatched me in. Honey, Squreball fled to de woods. I ain't never heard nothin' 'bout him. An' do you know, I didn't leave day 'oman's house no more for fifteen years?

Lord! Lord! honey, Squreball an' I use to sing dis song.

'Twas 1861, the Yankees made de Rebels run

We'll all go stone blin'

When de Johny's come a marchin' home.

Child an' here's another one we use to sing. 'Member de war done bin when we would sing dese songs. Listen now:

Ain't no more blowin' of dat fo' day horn

I will sing, brethern, I will sing.

A col' frosty mornin' de nigger's mighty good

Take your ax upon your shoulder.

Nigger talk to de woods,

Ain't no mor' blowin' of dat fo' day horn.

I will sing brethern, I will sing.

SONG

Kemo, Kimo, dar you are

Heh, ho rump to pume did'dle.

Set back pinkey wink,

Come Tom Nippecat

Sing song Kitty cat, can't

19

You carry me o'er?

2

Up de darkies head so bold

Sing song, Kitty, can't you

Carry me O'er?

Sing Song, Kitty, can't yo'

Carry me home?

I wuz at Pamplin an' de Yankees an' Rebels were fightin' an' dey were wavin' the bloody flag an' a confederate soldier wuz upon a post an' they were shootin' terribly. Guns were firin' everywhere.

All a sudden dey struck up Yankee Doodle Song. A soldier came along [HW: and] called to me, "How far is it to the Rebels", an I honey, wuz feared to tell him. So, I said, "I don't know". He called me again. Scared to death [HW: I was]. I recollect gittin' behind the house an' pointed in the direction. You see, ef de Rebels knew dat I told the soldier, they would have killed me.

These were the Union men goin' after Lee's army which had don' bin 'fore dem to Appomattox.

The Colored regiment came up behind an' when they saw the Colored regiment they put up the white flag. (Yo' 'member 'fo' dis red or bloody flag was up). Now, do you know why dey raised dat white flag? Well, honey, dat white flag wuz a token dat Lee, had surrendered. Glory! Glory! yes, child the Negroes are free, an' when they knew dat dey were free dey, Oh! Baby! began to sing:

Mamy don't yo' cook no mo',

Yo' ar' free, yo' ar' free.

Rooster don't yo' crow no mo',

Yo' ar' free, yo' ar' free.

Ol' hen, don't yo' lay no mo' eggs,

Yo' free, yo' free.

Sech rejoicing an' shoutin', you never he'rd in you' life.

Yes, I can recollect de blowin' up of the Crater. We had fled, but I do know 'bout the shellin' of Petersburg. We left Petersburg when de shellin' commenced an' went to Pamplin in box cars, gettin' out of de way. Dem were scared times too, cause you looked to be kilt any minute by stray bullets. Just before the shellin' of Petersburg, dey were sellin' niggers for little nothin' hardly.

3. FLORIDA FOLKLORE
SLAVE CUSTOMS AND ANECDOTES

MARY MINUS BIDDIE

Mary Minus Biddie, age one hundred five was born in Pensacola, Florida, 1833, and raised in Columbia County. She is married, and has several children. For her age she is exceptionally active, being able to wash and do her house work. With optimism she looks forward to many more years of life. Her health is excellent.

Having spent thirty-two years of her life as a slave she relates vividly some of her experiences.

Her master Lancaster Jamison was a very kind man and never mistreated his slaves. He was a man of mediocre means, and instead of having a large plantation as was usual in those days, he ran a boarding house, the revenue therefrom furnishing him substance for a livelihood. He had a small farm from which fresh produce was obtained to supply the needs of his lodgers. Mary's family were his only slaves. The family consisted of her mother, father, brother and a sister. The children called the old master "Fa" and their father "Pappy." The master never resented this appellation, and took it in good humor. Many travelers stopped at his boarding house; Mary's mother did the cooking, her father "tended" the farm, and Mary, her brother and sister, did chores about the place. There was a large one-room house built in the yard in which the family lived. Her father had a separate garden in which he raised his produce, also a smokehouse where the family meats were kept. Meats were smoked in order to preserve them.

During the day Mary's father was kept so busy attending his master's farm that there was no time for him to attend to a little farm that he was allowed to have. He overcame this handicap, however, by setting up huge scaffolds in the field which he burned and from the flames that this fire emitted he could see well enough to do what was necessary to his farm.

The master's first wife was a very kind woman; at her death Mary's master moved from Pensacola to Columbia County.

Mary was very active with the plow, she could handle it with the agility of a man. This prowess gained her the title of "plow girl."

COOKING

Stoves were unknown and cooking was done in a fireplace that was built of clay, a large iron rod was built in across the opening of the fireplace on which were hung pots that had special handles that fitted about the rod holding them in place over the blazing fire as the food cooking was done in a moveable oven which was placed in the fireplace over hot coals or corn cobs. Potatoes were roasted in ashes. Oft' times Mary's father would sit in front of the fireplace until a late hour in the night and on arising in the morning the children would find in a corner a number of roasted potatoes which their father had thoughtfully roasted and which the children readily consumed.

LIGHTING SYSTEM

Matches were unknown; a flint rock and a file provided the fire. This occured by striking a file against a flint rock which threw off sparks that fell into a wad of dry cotton used for the purpose. This cotton, as a rule, readily caught fire. This was fire and all the fire needed to start any blaze.

WEAVING

The white folk wove the cloth on regular looms which were made into dresses for the slaves. For various colors of cloth the thread was dyed. The dye was made by digging up red shank and wild indigo roots which were boiled. The substance obtained being some of the best dye to be found.

BEVERAGES & FOOD

Bread was made from flour and wheat. The meat used was pork, beef, mutton and goat. For preservation it was smoked and kept in the smokehouse. Coffee was used as a beverage and when this ran out as oft' times happened, parched peanuts were used for the purpose.

Mary and family arose before daybreak and prepared breakfast for the master and his family, after which they ate in the same dining room. When this was over the dishes were washed by Mary, her brother and sister. The children then played about until meals were served again.

WASHING and SOAP

Washing was done in home-made wooden tubs, and boiling in iron pots similar to those of today. Soap was made from fat and lye.

AMUSEMENTS

The only amusement to be had was a big candy pulling, or hog killing and chicken cooking. The slaves from the surrounding plantations were allowed to come together on these occasions. A big time was had.

CHURCH

The slaves went to the "white folks" church on Sundays. They were seated in the rear of the church. The white minister would arise and exhort the slaves to 'mind your masters, you owe them your respect.' An old Christian slave who perceived things differently could sometimes be heard to mumble, "Yeah, wese jest as good as deys is only deys white and we's black, huh." She dare not let the whites hear this. At times meetin's were held in a slave cabin where some "inspired" slave led the services.

In the course of years Mr. Jamison married again. His second wife was a veritable terror. She was always ready and anxious to whip a slave for the least misdemeanor. The master told Mary and her mother that before he would take the chance of them running away on account of her meanness he would leave her. As soon as he would leave the house this was a signal for his wife to start on a slave. One day, with a kettle of hot water in her hand, she chased Mary, who ran to another plantation and hid there until the good master returned. She then poured out her troubles to him. He was very indignant and remonstrated with his wife for being so cruel. She met her fate in later years; her son-in-law becoming angry at some of her doings in regard to him shot her, which resulted in her death. Instead of mourning, everybody seemed to rejoice, for the menace to well being had been removed. Twice a year Mary's father and master went to Cedar Keys, Florida to get salt. Ocean water was obtained and boiled, salt resulting. They always returned with about three barrels of salt.

The greatest event in the life of a slave was about to occur, and the most sorrowful in the life of a master, FREEDOM was at hand. A Negro was seen coming in the distance, mounted upon a mule, approaching Mr. Jamison who stood upon the porch. He told him of the liberation of the slaves. Mr. Jamison had never before been heard to curse, but this was one day that he let go a torrent of words that are unworthy to appear in print. He then broke down and cried like a slave who was being lashed by his cruel master. He called Mary's mother and father, Phyliss and Sandy, "I ain't got no more to do with you, you are free," he said, "if you want to stay with me you may and I'll give you one-third of what you raise." They decided to stay. When the crop was harvested the master did not do as he had promised. He gave them nothing. Mary slipped away, mounted the old mule "Mustang" and galloped away at a mules snail speed to Newnansville where she related what had happened to a Union captain. He gave her a letter to give to Mr. Jamison. In it he reminded him that if he didn't give Mary's family what he had promised he would be put in jail. Without hesitation the old master complied with these pungent orders.

After this incident Mary and her family left the good old boss to seek a new abode in other parts. This was the first time that the master had in any way displayed any kind of unfairness toward them, perhaps it was the reaction to having to liberate them.

MARRIAGE

There was no marriage during slavery according to civil or religious custom among the slaves. If a slave saw a woman whom he desired he told his master. If the woman in question belonged on another plantation, the master would consult her master: "one of my boys wants to marry one of your gals," he would say. As a rule it was agreeable that they should live together as man and wife. This was encouraged for it increased the slave population by new borns, hence, being an asset to the masters. The two slaves thus joined were allowed to see one another at intervals upon special permission from the master. He must have a pass to leave the plantation. Any slave caught without one while off the plantation was subject to be caught by the "paderollers" (a low class of white who roved the country to molest a slave at the least opportunity. Some of them were hired by the masters to guard against slaves running away or to apprehend them in the event that they did) who would beat them unmercifully, and send them back to the plantation from whence they came.

As a result of this form of matrimony at emancipation there were no slaves lawfully married. Orders were given that if they preferred to live together as man and wife they must marry according to law. They were given nine months to decide this question, after which if they continued to live together they were arrested for adultery. A Mr. Fryer, Justice of the Peace at Gainesville, was assigned to deal with the situation around the plantation where Mary and her family lived. A big supper was given, it was early, about twenty-five slave couples attended. There was gaiety and laughter. A barrel of lemonade was served. A big time was had by all, then those couples who desired to remain together were joined in wedlock according to civil custom. The party broke up in the early hours of the morning.

Mary Biddie, cognizant of the progress that science and invention has made in the intervening years from Emancipation and the present time, could not help but remark of the vast improvement of the lighting system of today and that of slavery. There were no lamps or kerosene. The first thread that shearer spun was for a wick to be used in a candle, the only means of light. Beef tallow was used to make the candle; this was placed in a candle mould while hot. The wick was then placed in the center of the tallow as it rest in the mould; this was allowed to cool. When this chemical process occured there was a regular sized candle to be used for lighting.

Mary now past the century mark, her lean bronze body resting in a rocker, her head wrapped in a white 'kerchief, and puffing slowly on her clay pipe, expressed herself in regard to presidents: "Roosevelt has don' mo' than any other president, why you know ever since freedom they been talkin' 'bout dis pension, talkin' 'bout it tha's all, but you see Mr. Roosevelt he don' com' an' gived it tu us. What? I'll say he's a good rightus man, an' um sho' go' vot' fo' him."

Residing in her little cabin in Eatonville, Florida, she is able to smile because she has some means of security, the Old Age Pension.

4. INTERVIEWER: MRS. BERNICE BOWDEN
PERSON INTERVIEWED: LETHA JOHNSON
2203 W. TWELFTH STREET, PINE BLUFF, ARKANSAS
Age: 77

"I heered the people say I was born in time of slavery. I was born durin' of the War.

"And when we went back home they said we had been freed four years.

"My father's last owner was named Crawford. He was a awful large man. That was in Monroe County, Mississippi.

"I know they was good to us 'cause we stayed right there after freedom till my father died in 1889. And mama stayed a year or two, then she come to Arkansas.

"After my husband died in 1919, I went to Memphis. Then this girl I raised— her mother willed her to me—I come here to Arkansas to live with her after I got down with the rheumatism so I couldn't wash and iron.

"In my husband's lifetime I didn't do nothin' but farm. And after I went to Memphis I cooked. Then I worked for a Italian lady, but she did her own cookin'. And oh, I thought she could make the best spaghetti.

"I used to spin and make soap. My last husband and I was married fifteen years and eight months and we never did buy a bar of soap. I used to be a good soap maker. And knit all my own socks and stockin's.

"I used to go to a school-teacher named Thomas Jordan. I remember he used to have us sing a song

'I am a happy bluebird

Sober as you see;

Pure cold water

Is the drink for me.

I'll take a drink here

And take a drink there,

Make the woods ring

With my temperance prayer.'

We'd all sing it; that was our school song. I believe that's the onliest one I can remember.

"'Bout this younger generation—well, I tell you, it's hard for me to say. It just puts me to a wonder. They gone a way back there. Seem like they don't have any 'gard for anything.

"I heard 'em 'fore I left Mississippi singin'

'Everybody's doin' it, doin' it.'

"'Co'se when I was young they was a few that was wild, but seem like now they is all wild. But I feels sorry for 'em."

5. FEDERAL WRITERS' PROJECT
AMERICAN GUIDE, (NEGRO WRITERS' UNIT)
CORA TAYLOR
FRANCES H. MINER, EDITOR
MIAMI, FLORIDA

RIVANA BOYNTON

[TR: also reported as Riviana.]

1. Where, and about when, were you born?

Sometime in 1850 on John and Mollie Hoover's plantation between Savannah and Charleston near the Georgia line.

2. If you were born on a plantation or farm, what sort of farming section was it in?

They raised rice, corn wheat, and lots of cotton, raised everything they et— vegetables, taters and all that.

3. How did you pass the time as a child? What sort of chores did you do and what did you play?

I had to thin cotton in the fields and mind the flies at the table. I chased them with a fly bush, sometimes a limb from a tree and sometimes wid a fancy bush.

4. Was your master kind to you?

Yes, I was favored by being with my massy.

5. How many slaves were there on the same plantation and farm?

I don't know. There was plenty o' dem up in de hundreds, I reckon.

6. Do you remember what kind of cooking utensils your mother used?

Yes, dey had spiders an' big iron kettles that dey hung in de chimney by a long chain. When dey wanted to cook fast dey lowered de chain and when dey wanted to bake in the spiders, they's put them under de kettle can cover with coals until dey was hot. Dey'd put de pones in does double concerned spiders and turn them around when dey was done on one side.

7. What were your main foods and how were they cooked?

We had everything you could think of to eat.

8. Do you remember making imitation or substitute coffee by grinding up corn or peanuts?

No. We had real coffee.

9. Do you remember ever having, when you were young, any other kind of bread besides corn bread?

Yes, batter and white bread.

10. Do you remember evaporating seawater to get salt?

[TR: word illegible] did hit dat way.

11. When you were a child, what sort of stove do you remember your mother having? Did they have a hanging pot in the fire place, and did they make their candles of their own tallow?

Always had fireplaces or open fires on the plantation, but after a long time while my massy had hearth stoves to cook on. De would give us slaves pot liquor to cook green in sometimes. Dey lit de fires with flint and steel, when it would go out. We all ate with wooden paddles for spoons. We made dem taller candles out of beef and mutton tallow, den we'd shoog 'em down into the candle sticks made of tin pans wid a handle on and a holder for the candle in the center. You know how.

12. Did you use an open well or pump to get the water?

We had a well with two buckets on a pulley to draw the water.

13. Do you remember when you first saw ice in regular form?

No. Ice would freeze in winter in our place.

14. Did your family work in the rice fields or in the cotton on the farm, or what sort of work did they do?

They did all kinds of work in the fields.

15. If they worked in the house or about the place, what sort of work did they do?

I was house maid and did everything they told me to do. Sometimes I'd sweep and work around all the time.

16. Do you remember ever helping tan and cure hides and pig hides?

This was done on the plantation. I took no part in it.

17. As a young person what sort of work did you do? If you helped your mother around the house or cut firewood or swept the yard, say so.

I helped do the housework and did what the mistress told me do.

18. When you were a child do you remember how people wove cloth, or spun thread, or picked out cotton seed, or weighed cotton or what sort of bag was used on the cotton bales?

No.

19. Do you remember what sort of soap they used? How did they get the lye for making the soap?

Yes, I'd help to make the ash lye and soft soap. Never seed and cake soap until I came here.

20. What did they use for dyeing thread and cloth and how did they dye them?

They used indigo for blue, copperas for yellow, and red oak chips for red.

21. Did your mother use big, wooden washtubs with cut-out holes on each side for the fingers?

Yes, and dey had smaller wooden keels. Never seed any tin tubs up there.

22. Do you remember the way they made shoes by hand in the country?

Yes, they made all our shoes on the plantation.

23. Do you remember saving the chicken feathers and goose feathers always for your featherbeds?

Yes.

23. Do you remember when women wore hoop [TR: illegible] in their skirts and when they stopped wearing them and wore narrow skirts?

Yes. My missus, she made me a pair of hoops, or I guess she bought it, but some of the slaves took thin limbs from trees and made their hoops. Others made them out of stiff paper and others would starch their skirts stiff with rice starch to make their skirts stand way out. We thought those hoops were just the thing for style.

25. Do you remember when you first saw your first windmill?

Yes. They didn't have them there.

26. Do you remember when you first saw bed springs instead of bed ropes?

I slept in a gunny bunk. My missus had a rope bed and she covered the ropes with a cow hide. We made hay and corn shuck mattresses for her. We'd cut the hay and shucks up fine and stuff the ticks with them. The cow hides were placed on top of the mattresses to protect them.

27. When did you see the first buggy and what did it look like?

It was a buggy like you see.

28. Do you remember your grandparents?

No. My mother was sold from me when I was small. I stayed in my uncle's shed at night.

29. Do you remember the money called "shin-plasters"?

No.

30. What interesting historical events happened during your youth, such as Sherman's army passing through your section? Did you witness the happenings and what was the reaction of the other Negroes to them?

I remember well when de war was on. I used to turn the big corn sheller and sack the shelled corn for the Confederate soldiers. They used to sell some of the corn and they gave some of it to the soldiers. Anyway the Yankees got some and they did not expect them to get it. It was this way: The Wheeler boys came through there ahead of Sherman's Army. Now, we thought the Wheeler boys were Confederates. They came down the road as happy as could be, a-singin'

6. INTERVIEW of FRANCES BATSON
1213 Scovel St.
NASHVILLE, TENNESSEE

"I dunno jes how ole I ez. I wuz baw'n 'yer in Nashville, durin' slabery. I must be way pas' 90 fer I member de Yankee soldiers well. De chilluns called dem de 'blue mans.' Mah white folks wuz named Crockett. Dr. Crockett wuz our marster but I don't member 'im mahse'f. He d'ed w'en I wuz small. Mah marster wuz mean ter mah mammy w'en her oler chilluns would run 'way. Mah oler br'er went ter war wid mah marster. Mah younger br'er run 'way, dey caught 'im, tuk 'im home en whup'd 'im. He run 'way en wuz nebber found."

"We wuzn't sold but mah mammy went 'way, en lef' me en I got up one mawnin' went ter mah mammy's room, she wuz gon'. I cried en cried fer her. Mah Missis wouldn't let me outa' de house, fer fear I'd try ter find her. Atter freedum mah br'er en a Yankee soldier kum in a waggin en git us. Mah white folks sed, I don' see why you ez takin' dez chilluns. Mah brudder said, 'We ez free now.' I member one whup'in mah missis gib me. Me en her daughter slipped 'way ter de river ter fish. We kotch a fish en mah missis had hit cooked fer us but whup'd us fer goin' ter de river."

"Whar de Buena Vista schul ez hit useter be a Yankee soldiers Barrick. Eber mawnin' dey hadder music. We chilluns would go on de hill, (whar the bag mill ez now) en listen ter dem. I member a black hoss de soldiers had, dat ef you called 'im Jeff Davis he would run you."

"I member de ole well on Cedar Street, neah de Capitol, en six mules fell in hit. Dat wuz back w'en blackberries wuz growin' on de Capitol Hill. En Morgan Park wuz called de pleasure gyarden. En hit wuz full ob Yankee soldiers. Atter de war dere wuz so many German peeple ober 'yer, dat fum Jefferson Street, ter Clay Street, wuz called Dutch town."

"I wuzn't bawn w'en de sta'rs fell. We didn't git nothin' w'en we wuz freed. Dunno much 'bout de Klu Klux Klan."

"Mah mammy useter tell me how de white folks would hire de slaves out ter mek money fer de marster en she tole me sum ob de marsters would hide dere slaves ter keep de Yankees fum gittin' dem."

"I don' b'leeve in white en black marriages. Mah sistah ma'ied a lite man. I wouldin' marry one ef hit would turn me ter gold. Dunno nothin' 'bout votin', allus tho't dat wuz fer de men."

"I can't think ob any tales er nuthin 'bout ghos'. 'Cept one 'bout a marster tyin' a nigger ter a fence en wuz beatin' 'im. A Yankee kum 'long made 'im untie de nigger en den de nigger beat de white man."

"Dis young peeples ez tough. I think half ob dem'll be hung, de way dey throw rocks at ole peoples. Dat's why I's crippled now, a white boy hit me wid a rock. I b'long ter de Methodist Chuch."

"Since freedum I'se hired out, washed en cooked fer diff'ent peeple. De only song I member: 'Hark Fum de Ground dis Mournful Sound.'"

7. FEDERAL WRITERS' PROJECT
AMERICAN GUIDE, (NEGRO WRITERS' UNIT)

PEARL RANDOLPH, FIELD WORKER
MADISON, FLORIDA
NOVEMBER 13, 1936

AMANDA MCCRAY

Mrs. McCray was sitting on her porch crooning softly to herself and rocking so gently that one might easily have thought the wind was swaying her chair. Her eyes were closed, her hands incredibly old and workworn were slowly folding and unfolding on her lap.

She listened quietly to the interviewer's request for some of the "high lights" of her life and finally exclaimed: "Chile, why'ny you look among the living fer the high lights?"

There was nothing resentful in this expression; only the patient weariness of one who has been dragged through the boundaries of a yesterday from which he was inseparable and catapulted into a present with which he has nothing in common. After being assured that her life story was of real interest to some one she warmed up and talked quite freely of the life and times as they existed in her day.

How old was she? She confessed quite frankly that she never "knowed" her age. She was a grownup during the Civil War when she was commandered by Union soldiers invading the country and employed as a cook. Her owner, one Redding Pamell, possessed a hundred or more slaves and was, according to her statement very kind to them. It was on his plantation that she was born. Amanda McCray is one of several children born to Jacob and Mary Williams, the latter being blind since Amanda could remember.

Children on the Pamell plantation led a carefree existence until they were about 12 years of age, when they were put to light chores like carrying

36

water and food, picking seed from cotton lint (there were no cotton gins), and minding the smaller children. They were duly schooled in all the current superstitions and listened to the tales of ghosts and animals that talked and reasoned, tales common to the Negro today. Little Mandy believes to this day that hogs can see the wind and that all animals talk like men on Christmas morning at a certain time. Children wore moles feet and pearl buttons around their necks to insure easy teething and had their legs bathed in a concoction of wasp nest and vinegar if they were slow about learning to walk. This was supposed to strengthen the weak limbs. It was a common occurence to see a child of two or three years still nursing at the mother's breast. Their masters encouraged the slaves to do this, thinking it made strong bones and teeth.

At Christmas time the slave children all trouped to "de big house" and stood outside crying "Christmas gift" to their master and mistress. They were never disappointed. Gifts consisted mostly of candies, nuts and fruits but there was always some useful article of clothing included, something they were not accustomed to having. Once little Mandy received a beautiful silk dress from her young mistress, who knew how much she liked beautiful clothes. She was a very happy child and loved the dress so much that she never wore it except on some special occasion.

Amanda was trained to be a house servant, learning to cook and knit from the blind mother who refused to let this handicap affect her usefulness. She liked best to sew the fine muslins and silks of her mistress, making beautiful hooped dresses that required eight and ten yards of cloth and sometimes as many as seven petticoats to enhance their fullness.

Hoops for these dresses were made of grape-vines that were shaped while green and cured in the sun before using. Beautiful imported laces were used to trim the petticoats and pantaloons of the wealthy.

The Pamell slaves had a Negro minister who could hold services any time he chose, so long as he did not interfere with the work of the other slaves. He was not obliged to do hard menial labors and went about the plantation "all dressed up" in a frock coat and store-bought shoes. He was more than a little conscious of this and was held in awe by the others. He often visited neighboring plantations to hold his services. It was from this minister that they first heard of the Civil War. He held whispered prayers for the success of the Union soldiers, not because freedom was so desirable to them, but for other slaves who were treated so cruelly. There was a praying ground where "the grass never had a chancet ter grow fer the troubled knees that kept it crushed down."

Amanda was an exceptionally good cook and so widespread was this knowledge that the Union soldiers employed her as a cook in their camp for a short while. She does not remember any of their officers and thinks they were no better nor worse than the others. These soldiers committed no depredations in her section except to confiscate whatever they wanted in the way of food and clothing. Some married southern girls.

Mr. Pamell made land grants to all slaves who wanted to remain with him; few left, so kind had he been to them all.

Life went on in much the same manner for Amanda's family except that the children attended school where a white teacher instructed them from a "blue back Webster." Amanda was a young woman but she managed to learn to read a little. Later they had colored teachers who followed much the same routine as the whites had. They were held in awe by the other Negroes and every little girl yearned to be a teacher, as this was about the only professional field open to Negro women at that time.

"After de war Negroes blossomed out with fine phaetons (buggies) and ceiled houses, and clothes—oh my!"

Mrs. McCray did not keep up with the politics of her time but remembers hearing about Joe Gibbs, member of the Florida Legislature. There was much talk then of Booker T. Washington, and many thought him a fool for trying to start a school in Alabama for Negroes. She recalls the Negro post master who served two or three terms at Madison. She could not give his name.

There have been three widespread "panics" (depressions) during her lifetime but Mrs. McCray thinks this is the worst one. During the Civil War, coffee was so dear that meal was parched and used as a substitute but now, she remarked, "you can't hardly git the meal for the bread."

Her husband and children are all dead and she lives with a niece who is no longer young herself. Circumstances are poor here. The niece earns her living as laundress and domestic worker, receiving a very poor wage. Mrs. McCray is now quite infirm and almost blind. She seems happiest talking of the past that was a bit kinder to her.

At present she lives on the northeast corner of First and Macon Streets. The post office address is #11, Madison, Florida.

REFERENCE

1. Personal interview with Amanda McCray, First and Macon Streets, Madison, Florida

8. INTERVIEW OF MRS. MINNIE FULKES
459 E. BYRNE STREET—PETERSBURG, VIRGINIA
BY—SUSIE BYRD
MARCH 5, 1937

I was born the twenty-fifth of December and I am 77 years old. My mother was a slave and she belonged to Dick Belcher in Chesterfield County. Old Dick sold us again to Gelaspe Graves. 'Member now fifteen of mother's chillun went with her having de same master.

Honey, I don't like to talk 'bout dem times, 'cause my mother did suffer misery. You know dar was an' overseer who use to tie mother up in de barn with a rope aroun' her arms up over her head, while she stood on a block. Soon as dey got her tied, dis block was moved an' her feet dangled, yo' know—couldn't tech de flo'.

Dis ol' man, now, would start beatin' her nekkid 'til the blood run down her back to her heels. I took an' seed th' whelps an' scars fer my own self wid dese here two eyes. (this whip she said, was a whip like dey use to use on horses); it wuz a piece of leather 'bout as wide as my han' from little finger to thumb. After dey had beat my muma all dey wanted another overseer. Lord, Lord, I hate white people and de flood waters gwine drown some mo. Well honey dis man would bathe her in salt and water. Don't you kno' dem places was a hurtin'. Um, um.

I asked mother what she done fer 'en to beat and do her so? She said, nothin', tother than she refused to be wife to dis man.

An' muma say, if he didn't treat her dis way a dozen times, it wasn't nary one.

Mind you, now muma's marster didn't know dis wuz going on. You know, if slaves would tell, why dem overseers would kill 'em.

An' she sed dat dey use to have meetings an' sing and pray an' th' ol' paddy rollers would hear dem, so to keep th' sound from goin' out, slaves would put a great big iron pot at the door, an' you know some times dey would fer git to put ol' pot dar an' the paddy rollers would come an' horse whip every las' one of 'em, jes cause poor souls were praying to God to free 'em from dat awful bondage.

Ha! ha! ha! dar wuz one ol' brudder who studied fer 'em one day an' tol all de slaves how to git even wid 'em.

He tol' 'em to tie grape vines an' other vines across th' road, den when de Paddy rollers come galantin' wid their horses runnin' so fast you see dem vines would tangle 'em up an' cause th' horses to stumble and fall. An' lots of times, badly dey would break dere legs and horses too; one interval one ol' poor devil got tangled so an' de horse kept a carryin' him, 'til he fell off horse and next day a sucker was found in road whar dem vines wuz wind aroun' his neck so many times yes had choked him, dey said, "He totely dead." Serve him right 'cause dem ol' white folks treated us so mean.

Well, sometimes, you know dey would, the others of 'em, keep going 'til dey fin' whar dis meeting wuz gwine on. Dey would come in and start whippin' an' beatin' the slaves unmerciful. All dis wuz done to keep yo' from servin' God, an' do you know some of dem devils wuz mean an' sinful 'nough to say, "Ef I ketch you here agin servin' God I'll beat you. You haven't time to serve God. We bought you to serve us." Um, um.

God's gwine 'rod dem wicket marsters. Ef hit 'taint 'em whut gits hit, hits gonna fall on deir chillun.

In dem back days child, meetings wuz carried on jes like we do today, somewhatly. Only difference is the slave dat knowed th' most 'bout de Bible would tell and explain what God had told him in a vision (yo' young folks say, "dream") dat dis freedom would come to pass; an' den dey prayed fer dis vision to come to pass, an' dars whar de paddy rollers would whip 'em ag'in.

Lord! Lord dey, pew! pew! pew! Baby, I jes kno' I could if I knowed how to write, an' had a little learning I could put off a book on dis here situation. Yo' kno what I mean 'bout dese way back questions yo' is a asking me to tell yo' 'bout; as fer as I can recallect in my mind.

When Graves bought us, he sold three of us an' three slaves. My brother an' sister went down south. Muma sed to de cotton country an' too, she say, "they were made to work in th' cotton fields by their new marster, out in dem white fields in th' brawlin' sun from th' time it breaked day 'till yo' couldn't see at night an', yes indeedy, an' if God isn't my right'ous judge they were given not half to eat, no not 'nough, to eat. Dey wuz beaten ef dey ask'd for any mo'".

As to marriage, when a slave wanted to marry, why he would jes ask his marster to go over and ask de tother marster could he take unto himself dis certain gal fer a wife. Mind you now, all de slaves dat marster called out of quarters an' he'd make 'em line up see, stand in a row like soldiers, and de slave man is wid his marster when dis askin' is gwine on, and he pulls de gal to him he wants; an' de marster den make both jump over broom stick an' after dey does, dey is prenounced man an' wife, both stayin' wid same marsters (I mean ef John marries Sallie, John stay wid his ol' marster an' Sal' wid hers, but had privileges, you know, like married folks; an' ef chillun were born all of 'em, no matter how many, belonged to de marster whar de woman stayed).

If I aint made a mistake, I think it wuz in April when de war surrendered an' muma an' all us wuz turned aloose in May. Yes dat ol' wench, a ol' heifer, oh child, it makes my blood bile when I think 'bout it. Yes she kept muma ig'runt. Didn't tell her nuthing 'bout being free 'til den in May.

Den her mistess, Miss Betsy Godsey, tol' her she wuz free, an' she (muma) coul' cook fer her jes th' same dat she would give her something to eat an' help clothe us chillun, dat wuz ef muma continual' to sta wid her an' work.

You see, we didn't have nuthin' an' no whar to go, um, um, um so we all, you know, jes took en stayed 'til we wuz able wid God's help to pull us selves together. But my God it wuz 'ginst our will, but, baby, couldn't help ourselves.

My fathers master tol' him he could farm one half fer th' tother an' when time rolled 'roun' fer dem 'viding crops he took an' give to him his part like any honest man would do. Ah, Lord child, dem wuz terrible times too, oh! it makes me shudder when I think of some slaves had to stay in de woods an' git long best way dey could after freedom done bin' clared; you see slaves who had mean master would rather be dar den whar dey lived. By an' by God opened a way an' dey got wid other slaves who had huts. You see, after th' render no white folks could keep slaves. Do yo' know even now, honey, an' dat done bin way bac' yonder, dese ol' white folks think us poor colored people is made to work an' slave fer dem, look! dey aint give you no wages worth nuthin'. Gal cook all week fer two an' three dollars. How can you live off it, how kin, how kin yo'?

My father waited on soldiers and after de s'render dey carried him an' his brother as fer as Washington D.C. I think we all use to say den, "Washington City." Aint you done heard folks talk 'bout dat city? 'Tis a grade big city, daus whar de President of dis here country stay; an' in bac' days it wuz known as 'vidin' lin' fer de North an' South. I done hear dem white folks tell all 'bout dem things—dis line. As I wuz tellin' you, his brother wuz kept, but dey sent father bac' home. Uncle Spencer wuz left in Prince Williams County. All his chillun ar' still dar. I don't know de name of Yankee who carried him off.

Lord, Lord, Honey, dem times too over sad, 'cause Yankees took lots of slaves away an' dey made homes. An' whole heap of families lost sight of each other. I know of a case whar after hit wuz ten years a brother an' sister lived side by side an' didn't know dey wuz blood kin.

My views 'bout de chillun in dem bac' days is dat dese here chillun what is now comin' up is too pizen brazen fer me.

No jes' lem me tell you how I did I married when I wuz 14 years old. So help me God, I didn't know what marriage meant. I had an idea when you loved de man, you an' he could be married an' his wife had to cook, clean up, wash, an' iron fer him was all. I slept in bed he on his side an' I on mine fer

Den muma said "Come here chillun," and she began tellin' me to please my husband, an' 'twas my duty as a wife, dat he had married a pu'fect lady.

Dese here chillun don't think of deir principle. Run purfectly wild. Old women too. Dey ain't all 'em true to one, but have two.

Jes what is gittin' into dis generation; is hit de worl' comin' to an end?

Ha! ha! ha! I goin' tel' yo' som'thin' else.

I had a young man to come to see me one evenin' an' he sed dis to me, "Miss Moore" "Let me jin my fence to your plantation."

I give him his hat. I say, "no" yo' go yo' way an' I go mine. I wuz through wid him, an' mind yo' I from dat da' 'til dis aint knowed what he wuz talkin' 'bout an' wuz ashamed to ask muma; but I thought he insulted me.

I didn't never go to school. Had to work an' am working now an' when hit breaks good weather, I go fishing. And who works dat big garden out dar? Nobody but me.

You know I'm mother of eleven chillun', an' 'tis seven living an' four of dem ded.

9. TEXAS EX-SLAVE NARRATIVE: MARY REYNOLDS: (BLACK RIVER, LOUISIANA)

Mary Reynolds claims to be more than a hundred years old. She was born in slavery to the Kilpatrick family, in Black River, Louisiana. Mary now lives at the Dallas County Convalescent Home. She has been blind for five years and is very feeble.

"My paw's name was Tom Vaughn and he was from the north, born free man and lived and died free to the end of his days. He wasn't no eddicated man, but he was what he calls himself a piano man. He told me once he lived in New York and Chicago and he built the insides of pianos and knew how to make them play in tune. He said some white folks from the south told he if he'd come with them to the south he'd find a lot of work to do with pianos in them parts, and he come off with them.

"He saw my maw on the Kilpatrick place and her man was dead. He told Dr. Kilpatrick, my massa, he'd buy my maw and her three chillun with all the money he had, iffen he'd sell her. But Dr. Kilpatrick was never one to sell any but the old niggers who was past workin' in the fields and past their breedin' times. So my paw marries my maw and works the fields, same as any other nigger. They had six gals: Martha and Pamela and Josephine and Ellen and Katherine and me.

"I was born same time as Miss Sara Kilpatrick. Dr. Kilpatrick's first wife and my maw come to their time right together. Miss Sara's maw died and they brung Miss Sara to suck with me. It's a thing we ain't never forgot. My maw's name was Sallie and Miss Sara allus looked with kindness on my maw. We sucked till we was a fair size and played together, which wasn't no common thing. None the other li'l niggers played with the white chillun. But Miss Sara loved me so good.

"I was jus' 'bout big 'nough to start playin' with a broom to go 'bout sweepin' up and not even half doin' it when Dr. Kilpatrick sold me. They was a old white man in Trinity and his wife died and he didn't have chick or child or slave or nothin'. Massa sold me cheap, 'cause he didn't want Miss Sara to play with no nigger young'un. That old man bought me a big doll and went off and left me all day, with the door open. I jus' sot on the floor and played with that doll. I used to cry. He'd come home and give me somethin' to eat and then go to bed, and I slep' on the foot of the bed with him. I was scart all the time in the dark. He never did close the door.

"Miss Sara pined and sickened. Massa done what he could, but they wasn't no pertness in her. She got sicker and sicker, and massa brung 'nother doctor. He say, 'You li'l gal is grievin' the life out her body and she sho' gwine die iffen you don't do somethin' 'bout it.' Miss Sara says over and over, 'I wants Mary.' Massa say to the doctor, 'That a li'l nigger young'un I done sold.' The doctor tells him he better git me back iffen he wants to save the life of his child. Dr. Kilpatrick has to give a big plenty more to git me back than what he sold me for, but Miss Sara plumps up right off and grows into fine health.

"Then massa marries a rich lady from Mississippi and they has chillun for company to Miss Sara and seem like for a time she forgits me.

"Massa Kilpatrick wasn't no piddlin' man. He was a man of plenty. He had a big house with no more style to it than a crib, but it could room plenty people. He was a medicine doctor and they was rooms in the second story for sick folks what come to lay in. It would take two days to go all over the land he owned. He had cattle and stock and sheep and more'n a hundred slaves and more besides. He bought the bes' of niggers near every time the spec'lators come that way. He'd make a swap of the old ones and give money for young ones what could work.

"He raised corn and cotton and cane and 'taters and goobers, 'sides the peas and other feedin' for the niggers. I 'member I helt a hoe handle mighty onsteady when they put a old woman to larn me and some other chillun to scrape the fields. That old woman would be in a frantic. She'd show me and then turn 'bout to show some other li'l nigger, and I'd have the young corn cut clean as the grass. She say, 'For the love of Gawd, you better larn it right, or Solomon will beat the breath out you body.' Old man Solomon was the nigger driver.

"Slavery was the worst days was ever seed in the world. They was things past tellin', but I got the scars on my old body to show to this day. I seed worse than what happened to me. I seed them put the men and women in the stock with they hands screwed down through holes in the board and they feets tied together and they naked behinds to the world. Solomon the overseer beat them with a big whip and massa look on. The niggers better not stop in the fields when they hear them yellin'. They cut the flesh most to the bones and some they was when they taken them out of stock and put them on the beds, they never got up again.

"When a nigger died they let his folks come out the fields to see him afore he died. They buried him the same day, take a big plank and bust it with a ax in the middle 'nough to bend it back, and put the dead nigger in betwixt it. They'd cart them down to the graveyard on the place and not bury them deep 'nough that buzzards wouldn't come circlin' round. Niggers mourns now, but in them days they wasn't no time for mournin'.

"The conch shell blowed afore daylight and all hands better git out for roll call or Solomon bust the door down and git them out. It was work hard, git beatin's and half fed. They brung the victuals and water to the fields on a slide pulled by a old mule. Plenty times they was only a half barrel water and it stale and hot, for all us niggers on the hottes' days. Mostly we ate pickled pork and corn bread and peas and beans and 'taters. They never was as much as we needed.

"The times I hated most was pickin' cotton when the frost was on the bolls. My hands git sore and crack open and bleed. We'd have a li'l fire in the fields and iffen the ones with tender hands couldn't stand it no longer, we'd run and warm our hands a li'l bit. When I could steal a 'tater, I used to slip it in the ashes and when I'd run to the fire I'd take it out and eat it on the sly.

"In the cabins it was nice and warm. They was built of pine boardin' and they was one long row of them up the hill back of the big house. Near one side of the cabins was a fireplace. They'd bring in two, three big logs and put on the fire and they'd last near a week. The beds was made out of puncheons fitted in holes bored in the wall, and planks laid 'cross them poles. We had tickin' mattresses filled with corn shucks. Sometimes the men build chairs at night. We didn't know much 'bout havin' nothin', though.

"Sometimes massa let niggers have a li'l patch. They'd raise 'taters or goobers. They liked to have them to help fill out on the victuals. 'Taters roasted in the ashes was the best tastin' eatin' I ever had. I could die better satisfied to have jus' one more 'tater roasted in hot ashes. The niggers had to work the patches at night and dig the 'taters and goobers at night. Then if they wanted to sell any in town they'd have to git a pass to go. They had to go at night, 'cause they couldn't ever spare a hand from the fields.

"Once in a while they'd give us a li'l piece of Sat'day evenin' to wash out clothes in the branch. We hanged them on the ground in the woods to dry. They was a place to wash clothes from the well, but they was so many niggers all couldn't git round to it on Sundays. When they'd git through with the clothes on Sat'day evenin's the niggers which sold they goobers and 'taters brung fiddles and guitars and come out and play. The others clap they hands and stomp they feet and we young'uns cut a step round. I was plenty biggity and liked to cut a step.

"We was scart of Solomon and his whip, though, and he didn't like frolickin'. He didn't like for us niggers to pray, either. We never heared of no church, but us have prayin' in the cabins. We'd set on the floor and pray with our heads down low and sing low, but if Solomon heared he'd come and beat on the wall with the stock of his whip. He'd say, 'I'll come in there and tear the hide off you backs.' But some the old niggers tell us we got to pray to

Gawd that he don't think different of the blacks and the whites. I know that Solomon is burnin' in hell today, and it pleasures me to know it.

"Once my maw and paw taken me and Katherine after night to slip to 'nother place to a prayin' and singin'. A nigger man with white beard told us a day am comin' when niggers only be slaves of Gawd. We prays for the end of Trib'lation and the end of beatin's and for shoes that fit our feet. We prayed that us niggers could have all we wanted to eat and special for fresh meat. Some the old ones say we have to bear all, 'cause that all we can do. Some say they was glad to the time they's dead, 'cause they'd rather rot in the ground than have the beatin's. What I hated most was when they'd beat me and I didn't know what they beat me for, and I hated them strippin' me naked as the day I was born.

"When we's comin' back from that prayin', I thunk I heared the nigger dogs and somebody on horseback. I say, 'Maw, its them nigger hounds and they'll eat us up.' You could hear them old hounds and sluts abayin'. Maw listens and say, 'Sho 'nough, them dogs am runnin' and Gawd help us!' Then she and paw talk and they take us to a fence corner and stands us up 'gainst the rails and say don't move and if anyone comes near, don't breathe loud. They went to the woods, so the hounds chase them and not git us. Me and Katherine stand there, holdin' hands, shakin' so we can hardly stand. We hears the hounds come nearer, but we don't move. They goes after paw and maw, but they circles round to the cabins and gits in. Maw say its the power of Gawd.

"In them days I weared shirts, like all the young'uns. They had collars and come below the knees and was split up the sides. That's all we weared in hot weather. The men weared jeans and the women gingham. Shoes was the worstes' trouble. We weared rough russets when it got cold, and it seem powerful strange they'd never git them to fit. Once when I was a young gal, they got me a new pair and all brass studs in the toes. They was too li'l for me, but I had to wear them. The brass trimmin's cut into my ankles and them places got mis'ble bad. I rubs tallow in them sore places and wrops rags round them and my sores got worser and worser. The scars are there to this day.

"I wasn't sick much, though. Some the niggers had chills and fever a lot, but they hadn't discovered so many diseases then as now. Dr. Kilpatrick give sick niggers ipecac and asafoetida and oil and turpentine and black fever pills.

"They was a cabin called the spinnin' house and two looms and two spinnin' wheels goin' all the time, and two nigger women sewing all the time. It took plenty sewin' to make all the things for a place so big. Once massa goes to Baton Rouge and brung back a yaller gal dressed in fine style. She was a seamster nigger. He builds her a house 'way from the quarters and she done fine sewin' for the whites. Us niggers knowed the doctor took a black woman quick as he did a white and took any on his place he wanted, and he took them often. But mostly the chillun born on the place looked like niggers. Aunt Cheyney allus say four of hers was massa's, but he didn't give them no mind. But this yaller gal breeds so fast and gits a mess of white young'uns. She larnt them fine manners and combs out they hair.

"Onct two of them goes down the hill to the doll house where the Kilpatrick chillun am playin'. They wants to go in the doll house and one the Kilpatrick boys say, 'That's for white chillun.' They say, 'We ain't no niggers, 'cause we got the same daddy you has, and he comes to see us near every day and fetches us clothes and things from town.' They is fussin' and Missy Kilpatrick is listenin' out her chamber window. She heard them white niggers say, 'He is our daddy and we call him daddy when he comes to our house to see our mama.'

"When massa come home that evenin' his wife hardly say nothin' to him, and he ask her what the matter and she tells him, 'Since you asks me, I'm studyin' in my mind 'bout them white young'uns of that yaller nigger wench from Baton Rouge.' He say, 'Now, honey, I fotches that gal jus' for you, 'cause she a fine seamster.' She say, 'It look kind of funny they got the same kind of hair and eyes as my chillun and they got a nose looks like yours.' He say, 'Honey, you jus' payin' 'tention to talk of li'l chillun that ain't got no mind to what they say.' She say, 'Over in Mississippi I got a home and plenty with my daddy and I got that in my mind.'

"Well, she didn't never leave and massa bought her a fine, new span of surrey hosses. But she don't never have no more chillun and she ain't so cordial with the massa. Margaret, that yellow gal, has more white young'uns, but they don't never go down the hill no more to the big house.

"Aunt Cheyney was jus' out of bed with a sucklin' baby one time, and she run away. Some say that was 'nother baby of massa's breedin'. She don't come to the house to nurse her baby, so they misses her and old Solomon gits the nigger hounds and takes her trail. They gits near her and she grabs a limb and tries to hist herself in a tree, but them dogs grab her and pull her down. The men hollers them onto her, and the dogs tore her naked and et the breasts plumb off her body. She got well and lived to be a old woman, but 'nother woman has to suck her baby and she ain't got no sign of breasts no more.

"They give all the niggers fresh meat on Christmas and a plug tobacco all round. The highes' cotton picker gits a suit of clothes and all the women what had twins that year gits a outfittin' of clothes for the twins and a double, warm blanket.

"Seems like after I got bigger, I 'member more'n more niggers run away. They's most allus cotched. Massa used to hire out his niggers for wage hands. One time he hired me and a nigger boy, Turner, to work for some ornery white trash name of Kidd. One day Turner goes off and don't come back. Old man Kidd say I knowed 'bout it, and he tied my wrists together and stripped me. He hanged me by the wrists from a limb on a tree and spraddled my legs round the trunk and tied my feet together. Then he beat me. He beat me worser than I ever been beat before and I faints dead away. When I come to I'm in bed. I didn't care so much iffen I died.

"I didn't know 'bout the passin' of time, but Miss Sara come to me. Some white folks done git word to her. Mr. Kidd tries to talk hisself out of it, but Miss Sara fotches me home when I'm well 'nough to move. She took me in a cart and my maw takes care of me. Massa looks me over good and says I'll git well, but I'm ruint for breedin' chillun.

"After while I taken a notion to marry and massa and missy marries us same as all the niggers. They stands inside the house with a broom held crosswise of the door and we stands outside. Missy puts a li'l wreath on my head they kept there and we steps over the broom into the house. Now, that's all they was to the marryin'. After freedom I gits married and has it put in the book by a preacher.

"One day we was workin' in the fields and hears the conch shell blow, so we all goes to the back gate of the big house. Massa am there. He say, 'Call the roll for every nigger big 'nough to walk, and I wants them to go to the river and wait there. They's gwine be a show and I wants you to see it.' They was a big boat down there, done built up on the sides with boards and holes in the boards and a big gun barrel stickin' through every hole. We ain't never seed nothin' like that. Massa goes up the plank onto the boat and comes out on the boat porch. He say, 'This am a Yankee boat.' He goes inside and the water wheels starts movin' and that boat goes movin' up the river and they says it goes to Natches.

"The boat wasn't more'n out of sight when a big drove of sojers comes into town. They say they's Fed'rals. More'n half the niggers goes off with them sojers, but I goes on back home 'cause of my old mammy.

"Next day them Yankees is swarmin' the place. Some the niggers wants to show them somethin'. I follows to the woods. The niggers shows them sojers a big pit in the ground, bigger'n a big house. It is got wooden doors that lifts up, but the top am sodded and grass growin' on it, so you couldn't tell it. In that pit is stock, hosses and cows and mules and money and chinaware and silver and a mess of stuff them sojers takes.

"We jus' sot on the place doin' nothin' till the white folks comes home. Miss Sara come out to the cabin and say she wants to read a letter to my mammy. It come from Louis Carter, which is brother to my mammy, and he done follow the Fed'rals to Galveston. A white man done write the letter for him. It am tored in half and massa done that. The letter say Louis am workin' in Galveston and wants mammy to come with us, and he'll pay our way. Miss Sara say massa swear, 'Damn Louis Carter. I ain't gwine tell Sallie nothin',' and he starts to tear the letter up. But she won't let him, and she reads it to mammy.

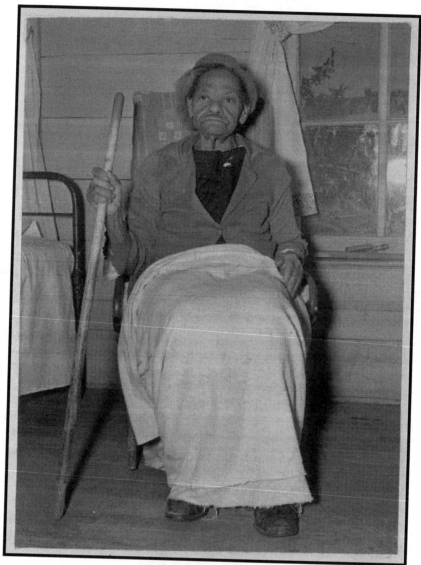

Mary Reynolds

After a time massa takes all his niggers what wants to Texas with him and mammy gits to Galveston and dies there. I goes with massa to the Tennessee Colony and then to Navasota. Miss Sara marries Mr. T. Coleman and goes to El Paso. She wrote and told me to come to her and I allus meant to go.

"My husband and me farmed round for times, and then I done housework and cookin' for many years. I come to Dallas and cooked seven year for one white family. My husband died years ago. I guess Miss Sara been dead these long years. I allus kep' my years by Miss Sara's years, 'count we is born so close.

"I been blind and mos' helpless for five year. I'm gittin' mighty enfeeblin' and I ain't walked outside the door for a long time back. I sets and 'members the times in the world. I 'members now clear as yesterday things I forgot for a long time. I 'members 'bout the days of slavery and I don't 'lieve they ever gwine have slaves no more on this earth. I think Gawd done took that burden offen his black chillun and I'm aimin' to praise him for it to his face in the days of Glory what ain't so far off."

10. MILLIE RANDALL
ENSLAVED AT THE DAN MCMILLAN FARM, NEAR BIG CANE, LOUISIANA.

Millie Randall, was born in Mississippi, but spent most of her slavery days on the Dan McMillan farm, near Big Cane, Louisiana. She is about 80 years old, though her estimate of her actual age is vague. She now lives in Beaumont, Texas.

"I was jes' 'bout six year old when peace was 'clared and I done been born in Mississippi, but us move to Bayou Jacques, tother side of Big Cane, in Louisiana. I mus' be purty old now.

"My name' Millie Randall and my mammy, she call' Rose, but I don't know nothin' 'bout my paw. My old massa name' Dan McMillan and he wife she name' Laura. It were a old wood country where my white folks was and us live way out. Dey raise de corn and de cotton and when dey wasn't workin' in de field, dey diggin' out stumps and movin' logs and clearin' up new ground. Dey have lots of goats and sheep, too, and raises dey own rice.

"Dey give us cullud folks de ration in a sack right reg'lar. It have jes' plain food in it, but plenty for everybody.

"Missy have de big plank house and us have de little log house. Us have jes' old plank beds and no furniture. Us clothes make out good, strong cloth, but dey was plain make.

"All us white folks was mean, I tells you de truf. Yes, Lawd, I seed dem beat and almost kilt on us own place. What dey beat dem for? 'Cause dey couldn't he'p demselves, I guess. De white folks have de niggers like dey want dem and dey treat dem bad. It were de old, bully, mean overseers what was doin' de beatin' up with de niggers and I guess dey would have kilt me, but I's too little to beat much.

"I heered 'bout dem Yankees drivin' dey hosses in de white folks' house and makin' dem let dem eat offen de table. Another time, dey come to de plantation and all de niggers locked in de barn. Dose soldiers go in de house and find de white boss man hidin' in 'tween de mattresses and dey stick swords through de mattress and kilt him.

Millie Randall

"Some de white folks hides dey silver and other things that worth lots of money and hang dem down in de well, so de Yankees not find dem. But dey find dem anyway. Dey breaks open a store what was lock up and told de niggers to git all dey wants. De women ketches up de bottom of dey skirt round de waist and fill dem up with everything dey wants.

"After freedom old massa not 'low my mammy have us chillen. He takes me and my brother, Benny, in de wagon and druv us round and round so dey couldn't find us. My mammy has to git de Jestice of de Peace to go make him turn us a-loose. He brung us to our mammy and was we glad to see her.

"I don't 'member 'xactly when I git marry. It was at Big Cane and when I git marry I jes' git marry, dat's all. Dey was three chillen but dey all dead now and so my husban'."

11. TEXAS EX-SLAVE NARRATIVE OF HAGAR LEWIS

HAGAR LEWIS, tall and erect at 82 years of age, lives at 4313 Rosa St., El Paso, Texas. She was born a slave of the Martin family and was given with her mother and family to Mary Martin, when she married John M. McFarland. They lived near Tyler, Smith Co., Texas. When freed she remained with the McFarlands until she married A. Lewis and moved to San Antonio, Texas. Widowed early, she raised two sons. One, chief electrical engineer with the U.S. government, lives in New York City. He provides for his aged mother.

[HW: Illegible]

"I was born Jan. 12th, 1855. My first owners was the Martins, and when their daughter, Mary, married, I was give to her. My mama lived to 112 years old. She had sixteen children. I was the baby.

"Missus Mary McFarland, my mother's missus and mine, taught us children with her own; learned us how to read and write. She treated us just like we were her children. We had very strict leaders, my mother and Missus Mary. She'd say, 'Mammy Lize (my mother), 'you'll have to come and whop Oscar and Hagar, they's fightin!' Mammy Lize would say, 'No, I won't whop 'em, I'll just punish 'em.' And we'd have to stand with our backs to each other. My missus never did much whoppin'.

"We lived in cabins made of logs and chinked with mud mortar. We had beds that had only one leg; they fit in each corner of the walls. They was strong, stout. We could jump on 'em and have lots of fun. We didn' stay in quarters much. The cabins was near a creek where willows grew and we'd make stick horses out of 'em. We called it our horse lot. On the farm was a spring that threw water high, and we'd go fishing in a big lake on one corner of the farm. Marster owned half a league, maybe more.

"I was 12 years old when freed. I can remember the way my marster come home from the war. The oldest son, Oscar, and I was out in the yard, and I saw marster first, comin' down the road, and I hollered and screamed, 'O, Oscar, Marse John's a-comin! Marse John's a-comin' home!' We stayed on with them 'till they all died off but Oscar.

"We never changed our name 'till after the Civil War. Then Marse John said, 'Mammy Lize, you gotta choose a name.' He carried us into Tyler to a bureau or something. Mammy Lize say, 'I'm going to keep the name McFarland. I ain't got no other name.'

"My father was a slave from another farm. My mother was the cook. She cooked it all in the same place for white folks and us. We ate the same, when the white folks was finished. They's a big light bread oven in the yard of the big house and in front of the quarters, under a big tree. That one baked the pies. The cabins had a big fireplace wider than that piano there. They'd hang meat and sausage and dry them in the fireplace. Cut holes in ham and hang them there. Had big hogsheads filled up with flour, corn and wheat.

"Some pore niggers were half starved. They belonged to other people. Missus Mary would call them in to feed 'em, see 'em outside the fence pickin' up scraps. They'd call out at night, 'Marse John, Marse John.' They's afraid to come in daytime. Marse John'd say, 'What's the matter now?' They'd say, 'I'se hongry.' He'd say, 'Come in and git it.' He'd cure lots of meat, for we'd hear 'em hollerin' at night when they'd beat the pore niggers for beggin' or stealin', or some crime.

"Marse John would saddle up Old Charlie and go see. He had a big shot gun across his lap. We'd hear that ole bull whip just a poppin'. They'd turn 'em loose when Marse John got after 'em. He prosecuted some marsters for beatin' the slaves. He knew they was half feedin' 'em. One time he let us go see where they'd drug two niggers to death with oxen. For stealin' or somethin'. I can't say we were treated bad, 'cause I'd tell a story. I've always been treated good by whites, but many of the niggers was killed. They'd say bad words to the bosses and they'd shoot 'em. We'd ask Miss Mary why did they kill old Uncle so and so, and Miss Mary would say, 'I don't know. It's not right to say when you don't know.' I'm glad to see slavery over.

"When I was turned loose Miss Mary was training me and sister to do handwork, knittin' and such. Mama wouldn't let us dance, didn't want any rough children. Miss Mary'd say, when I'd get sleepy, 'Owl eyes, ain't you sleepy?' I'd say, 'No, ma'am, anything you want us to do?' I cried to sleep in the big house with Miss Mary and the children, 'cause my sister Belle did. Said she's goin' to turn white 'cause she stayed with the white folks, and I wanted to turn white, too.

"Miss Mary'd make our Sunday dresses. My mother put colored thread in woven material and they was pretty. We had plenty of clothes. Miss Mary saw to that. They paid my mother for every child she had that was big enough to work, and Marse John saw that others did the same.

"Some whites had a dark hole in the ground, a 'dungeon,' they called it, to put their slaves in. They'd carry 'em bread and water once a day. I'se afraid of the hole, they'd tell me the devil was in that hole.

Hagar Lewis

"We set traps for 'possum, coons and squirrels. We used to have big sport ridin' goats. One near bustcd me wide open. Miss Mary's brother put me on it, and they punished him good for it. He didn't get to play for a long time.

And we had an old buck sheep. He'd keep Oscar and I up on the oak patch fence all the time.

"We'd watch the doodle bugs build their houses. We'd sing, 'Doodle, Doodle, your house burned down.' Those things would come up out of their holes just a-shakin'.

"One game I remember was, 'Skip frog, Skip frog, Answer your Mother, she's callin' you, you, you.' We'd stand in a circle and one would be skip frog. We'd slap our hands and skip frog would be hoppin' just like frogs do. Oh, I wish I could call them times back again. I'd go back tomorrow. But I'm tryin' to live so I can meet 'em once again."

12. [HW: Dist 1 Ex-Slave #62]

GEORGIA EX-SLAVE INTERVIEW:
EMMALINE KILPATRICK, Age 74
Born a slave on the plantation of Judge William Watson Moore,
WHITE PLAINS, (GREENE COUNTY) GEORGIA

BY: SARAH H. HALL
ATHENS, GA.
[Date Stamp: MAY 8 1937]

One morning in October, as I finished planting hyacinth bulbs on my cemetery lot, I saw an old negro woman approaching. She was Emmaline Kilpatrick, born in 1863, on my grandfather's plantation.

"Mawnin' Miss Sarah," she began, "Ah seed yer out hyar in de graveyard, en I cum right erlong fer ter git yer ter read yo' Aunt Willie's birthday, offen her toomstone, en put it in writin' fer me."

"I don't mind doing that for you, Emmaline," I replied, "but why do you want to know my aunt's birthday?"

"Well," answered the old ex-slave, "I can't rightly tell mah age no udder way. My mammy, she tole me, I wuz bawned de same night ez Miss Willie wuz, en mammy allus tole me effen I ever want ter know how ole I is, jes' ask my white folks how ole Miss Willie is."

When I had pencilled the birthdate on a scrap of paper torn from my note book and she had tucked it carefully away in a pocket in her clean blue checked gingham apron, Emmaline began to talk of the old days on my grandfather's farm.

"Miss Sarah, Ah sho did love yo' aunt Willie. We wuz chilluns growin' up tergedder on Marse Billie's place. You mought not know it, but black chilluns gits grown heap faster den white chilluns, en whilst us played 'round de yard, en orchards, en pastures out dar, I wuz sposed ter take care er Miss Willie en not let her git hurt, er nuthin' happen ter her."

65

"My mammy say dat whan Marse Billie cum hom' frum de War, he call all his niggers tergedder en tell 'am dey is free, en doan b'long ter nobody no mo'. He say dat eny uf 'um dat want to, kin go 'way and live whar dey laks, en do lak dey wanter. Howsome ebber, he do say effen enybody wants ter stay wid him, en live right on in de same cabins, dey kin do it, effen dey promise him ter be good niggers en mine him lak dey allus done."

"Most all de niggers stayed wid Marse Billie, 'ceppen two er thee brash, good fer nuthin's."

Standing there in the cemetery, as I listened to old Emmaline tell of the old days, I could see cotton being loaded on freight cars at the depot. I asked Emmaline to tell what she could remember of the days whan we had no railroad to haul the cotton to market.

"Well," she said, "Fore dis hyar railroad wuz made, dey hauled de cotton ter de Pint (She meant Union Point) en sold it dar. De Pint's jes' 'bout twelve miles fum hyar. Fo' day had er railroad thu de Pint, Marse Billie used ter haul his cotton clear down ter Jools ter sell it. My manny say dat long fo' de War he used ter wait twel all de cotton wuz picked in de fall, en den he would have it all loaded on his waggins. Not long fo' sundown he wud start de waggins off, wid yo' unker Anderson bossin' 'em, on de all night long ride towards Jools. 'Bout fo' in de mawnin' Marse Billie en yo' grammaw, Miss Margie, 'ud start off in de surrey, driving de bays, en fo' dem waggins git ter Jools Marse Billie done cotch up wid em. He drive er head en lead em on ter de cotton mill in Jools, whar he sell all his cotton. Den him en Miss Margie, dey go ter de mill sto' en [011] buy white sugar en udder things dey doan raise on de plantation, en load 'em on de waggins en start back home."

"But Emmaline," I interrupted, "Sherman's army passed through Jewels and burned the houses and destroyed the property there. How did the people market their cotton then?"

Emmaline scratched her head. "Ah 'members somepin 'bout dat," she declared. "Yassum, I sho' does 'member my mammy sayin' dat folks sed when de Fed'rals wuz bunnin' up evvy thing 'bout Jools, dey wuz settin' fire ter de mill, when de boss uv dem sojers look up en see er sign up over er upstairs window. Hit wuz de Mason's sign up day, kaze dat wuz de Mason's lodge hall up over de mill. De sojer boss, he meks de udder sojers put out de

66

fire. He say him er Mason hisself en he ain' gwine see nobuddy burn up er Masonic Hall. Dey kinder tears up some uv de fixin's er de Mill wuks, but dey dassent burn down de mill house kaze he ain't let 'em do nuthin' ter de Masonic Hall. Yar knows, Miss Sarah, Ah wuz jes' 'bout two years ole when dat happen, but I ain't heered nuffin' 'bout no time when dey didden' take cotton ter Jools ever year twel de railroad come hyar."

"Did yer ax me who mah'ed my maw an paw? Why, Marse Billie did, cose he did! He wuz Jedge Moore, Marse Billie wuz, en he wone gwine hev no foolis'mant 'mongst 'is niggers. Fo' de War en durin' de War, de niggers went ter de same church whar dare white folks went. Only de niggers, dey set en de gallery."

"Marse Billie made all his niggers wuk moughty hard, but he sho' tuk good keer uv 'em. Miss Margie allus made 'em send fer her when de chilluns wuz bawned in de slave cabins. My mammy, she say, Ise 'bout de onliest slave baby Miss Margie diden' look after de bawnin, on dat plantation. When any nigger on dat farm wuz sick, Marse Billie seed dat he had medicine an lookin' atter, en ef he wuz bad sick Marse Billie had da white folks doctor come see 'bout 'im."

"Did us hev shoes? Yas Ma'am us had shoes. Dat wuz all ole Pegleg wuz good fer, jes ter mek shoes, en fix shoes atter dey wuz 'bout ter give out. Pegleg made de evvy day shoes for Marse Billie's own chilluns, 'cept now en den Marse Billie fetched 'em home some sto' bought shoes fun Jools."

"Yassum, us sho' wuz skeered er ghosts. Dem days when de War won't long gone, niggers sho' wus skert er graveyards. Mos' evvy nigger kep' er rabbit foot, kaze ghosties wone gwine bodder nobuddy dat hed er lef' hind foot frum er graveyard rabbit. Dem days dar wuz mos' allus woods 'round de graveyards, en it uz easy ter ketch er rabbit az he loped outer er graveyard. Lawsy, Miss Sarah, dose days Ah sho' wouldn't er been standin' hyar in no graveyard talkin' ter ennybody, eben in wide open daytime."

"En you ax wuz dey enny thing else uz wuz skert uv? Yassum, us allus did git moughty oneasy ef er scritch owl hollered et night. Pappy ud hop right out er his bed en stick de fire shovel en de coals. Effen he did dat rat quick, an look over 'is lef' shoulder whilst de shovel gittin' hot, den maybe no no nigger gwine die dat week on dat plantation. En us nebber did lak ter fine er hawse tail hair en de hawse trough, kaze us wuz sho' ter meet er snake fo' long."

"Yassum, us had chawms fer heap er things. Us got 'em fum er ole Injun 'oman dat lived crost de crick. Her sold us chawms ter mek de mens lak us, en chawms dat would git er boy baby, er anudder kind er chawms effen yer want er gal baby. Miss Margie allus scold 'bout de chawns, en mek us shamed ter wear 'em, 'cept she doan mine ef us wear asserfitidy chawms ter keep off fevers, en she doan say nuffin when my mammy wear er nutmeg on a wool string 'round her neck ter keep off de rheumatiz.

"En is you got ter git on home now, Miss Sarah? Lemme tote dat hoe en trowel ter yer car fer yer. Yer gwine ter take me home in yer car wid yer, so ez I kin weed yer flower gyarden fo' night? Yassum, I sho' will be proud ter do it fer de black dress you wo' las' year. Ah gwine ter git evvy speck er grass outer yo' flowers, kaze ain' you jes' lak yo' grammaw—my Miss Margie."

13. [HW: Dist 5 Ex-Slave #63]

Whitley,
1-22-36
Driskell, GA

GEORGIA EX SLAVE JENNIE KENDRICKS
[Date Stamp: MAY 8 1937]

JENNIE KENDRICKS, the oldest of 7 children, was born in Sheram, Georgia in 1855. Her parents were Martha and Henry Bell. She says that the first thing she remembers is being whipped by her mother.

Jennie Kendricks' grandmother and her ten children lived on this plantation. The grandmother had been brought to Georgia from Virginia: "She used to tell me how the slave dealers brought her and a group of other children along much the same as they would a herd of cattle," said the ex-slave, "when they reached a town all of them had to dance through the streets and act lively so that the chances for selling them would be greater".

When asked to tell about Mr. Moore, her owner, and his family Jennie Kendricks stated that although her master owned and operated a large plantation, he was not considered a wealthy man. He owned only two other slaves besides her immediate family and these were men.

"In Mr. Moores family were his mother, his wife, and six children (four boys and two girls). This family lived very comfortably in a two storied weatherboard house. With the exception of our grandmother who cooked for the owner's family and slaves, and assisted her mistress with housework all the slaves worked in the fields where they cultivated cotton and the corn, as well as the other produce grown there. Every morning at sunrise they had to get up and go to the fields where they worked until it was too dark to see. At noon each day they were permitted to come to the kitchen, located just a short distance in the rear of the master's house, where they were served dinner. During the course of the day's work the women shared all the men's work except plowing. All of them picked cotton when it was time to gather the crops. Some nights they were required to [002] spin and to help Mrs. Moore, who did all of the weaving. They used to do their own personal work,

69

at night also." Jennie Kendricks says she remembers how her mother and the older girls would go to the spring at night where they washed their clothes and then left them to dry on the surrounding bushes.

As a little girl Jennie Kendricks spent all of her time in the master's house where she played with the young white children. Sometimes she and Mrs. Moore's youngest child, a little boy, would fight because it appeared to one that the other was receiving more attention from Mrs. Moore than the other. As she grew older she was kept in the house as a playmate to the Moore children so she never had to work in the field a single day.

She stated that they all wore good clothing and that all of it was made on the plantation with one exception. The servants spun the thread and Mrs. Moore and her daughters did all of the weaving as well as the making of the dresses that were worn on this particular plantation. "The way they made this cloth", she continued, "was to wind a certain amount of thread known as a "cut" onto a reel. When a certain number of cuts were reached they were placed on the loom. This cloth was colored with a dye made from the bark of trees or with a dye that was made from the indigo berry cultivated on the plantation. The dresses that the women wore on working days were made of striped or checked materials while those worn on Sunday were usually white."

She does not know what the men wore on work days as she never came in contact with them. Stockings for all were knitted on the place. The shoes, which were the one exception mentioned above, were made by one Bill Jacobs, an elderly white man who made the shoes for all the plantations in the community. The grown people wore heavy shoes called "Brogans" while those worn by the children were not so heavy and were called "Pekers" because of their narrow appearance. For Sunday wear, all had shoes bought for this purpose. Mr. Moore's mother was a tailoress and at times, when the men were able to get the necessary material, she made their suits.

There was always enough feed for everybody on the Moore plantation. Mrs. Moore once told Jennie's mother to always see that her children had sufficient to eat so that they would not have to steal and would therefore grow up to be honorable. As the Grandmother did all of the cooking, none of the other servants ever had to cook, not even on Sundays or other holidays such as the Fourth of July. There was no stove in this plantation kitchen, all the cooking was done at the large fireplace where there were a number of hooks called potracks. The pots, in which the cooking was done, hung from these hooks directly over the fire.

The meals served during the week consisted of vegetables, salt bacon, corn bread, pot liquor, and milk. On Sunday they were served milk, biscuits, vegetables, and sometimes chicken. Jennie Kendricks ate all of her meals in the master's house and says that her food was even better. She was also permitted to go to the kitchen to get food at any time during the day. Sometimes when the boys went hunting everyone was given roast 'possum and other small game. The two male slaves were often permitted to accompany them but were not allowed to handle the guns. None of the slaves had individual gardens of their own as food sufficient for their needs was raised in the master's garden.

The houses that they lived in were one-roomed structures made of heavy plank instead of logs, with planer [HW: ?] floors. At one end of this one-roomed cabin there was a large chimney and fireplace made of rocks, mud, and dirt. In addition to the one door, there was a window at the back. Only one family could live in a cabin as the space was so limited. The furnishings of each cabin consisted of a bed and one or two chairs. The beds were well constructed, a great deal better than some of the beds the ex-slave saw during these days. Regarding mattresses she said, "We took some tick and stuffed it with cotton and corn husks, which had been torn into small pieces and when we got through sewing it looked like a mattress that was bought in a store."

Light was furnished by lightwood torches and sometimes by the homemade tallow candles. The hot tallow was poured into a candle mold, which was then dipped into a pan of cold water, when the tallow had hardened, the finished product was removed.

Whenever there was sickness, a doctor was always called. As a child Gussie was rather sickly, and a doctor was always called to attend to her. In addition to the doctor's prescriptions there was heart leaf tea and a warm remedy of garlic tea prepared by her grandmother.

If any of the slaves ever pretended sickness to avoid work, she knows nothing about it.

As a general rule, slaves were not permitted to learn to read or write, but the younger Moore children tried to teach her to spell, read, and write. When she used to stand around Mrs. Moore when she was sewing she appeared to be interested and so she was taught to sew.

Every Sunday afternoon they were all permitted to go to town where a colored pastor preached to them. This same minister performed all marriages after the candidates had secured the permission of the master.

There was only one time when Mr. Moore found it necessary to sell any of his slaves. On this occasion he had to sell two; he saw that they were sold to another kind master.

The whipping on most plantation were administered by the [HW: over]seers and in some cases punishment was rather severe. There was no overseer on this plantation. Only one of Mr. Moore's sons told the field hands what to do. When this son went to war it became necessary to hire an overseer. Once he attempted to whip one of the women but when she refused to allow him to whip her he never tried to whip any of the others. Jennie Kendricks' husband, who was also a slave, once told her his master was so mean that he often whipped his slaves until blood ran in their shoes.

There was a group of men, known as the "Patter-Rollers", whose duty it was to see that slaves were not allowed to leave their individual plantations without passes which [HW: they] were supposed to receive from their masters. "A heap of them got whippings for being caught off without these passes," she stated, adding that "sometimes a few of them were fortunate enough to escape from the Patter-Rollers". She knew of one boy who, after having outrun the "Patter-Rollers", proceeded to make fun of them after he was safe behind his master's fence. Another man whom the Patter-Rollers had pursued any number of times but who had always managed to escape, was finally caught one day and told to pray before he was given his whipping. As he obeyed he noticed that he was not being closely observed, whereupon he made a break that resulted in his escape from them again.

The treatment on some of the other plantations was so severe that slaves often ran away, Jennie Kendricks told of one man [HW: who was] [TR: "being" crossed out] lashed [HW: and who] ran away but was finally caught. When his master brought him back he was locked in a room until he could be punished. When the master finally came to administer the whipping, Lash had cut his own throat in a last effort to secure his freedom. He was not successful; his life was saved by quick action on the part of his master. Sometime later after rough handling Lash finally killed his master [HW: and] was burned at the stake for this crime.

Other slaves were more successful at escape, some being able to remain away for as long as three years at a time. At nights, they slipped to the plantation where they stole hogs and other food. Their shelters were usually caves, some times holes dug in the ground. Whenever they were caught, they were severely whipped.

A slave might secure his freedom without running away. This is true in the case of Jennie Kendricks' grandfather who, after hiring his time out for a number of years, was able to save enough money with which to purchase himself from his master.

Jennie Kendricks remembers very little of the talk between her master and mistress concerning the war. She does remember being taken to see the Confederate soldiers drill a short distance from the house. She says "I though it was very pretty, 'course I did'nt know what was causing this or what the results would be". Mr. Moore's oldest sons went to war [HW: but he] himself did not enlist until the war was nearly over. She was told that the Yankee soldiers burned all the gin houses and took all live stock that they saw while on the march, but no soldiers passed near their plantation.

After the war ended and all the slaves had been set free, some did not know it, [HW: as] they were not told by their masters. [HW: A number of them] were tricked into signing contracts which bound them to their masters for several years longer.

As for herself and her grandmother, they remained on the Moore property where her grandmother finally died. Her mother moved away when freedom was declared and started working for someone else. It was about this time that Mr. Moore began to prosper, he and his brother Marvin gone into business together.

According to Jennie Kendricks, she has lived to reach such a ripe old age because she has always been obedient and because she has always been [007] a firm believer in God.

14. GARRARD COUNTY. KENTUCKY EX-SLAVE STORIES.
(Eliza Ison) [HW: Ky 11]

SUBJECT INTERVIEWED:
AUNT HARRIET MASON—EX-SLAVE:

She was born one mile below Bryantsville on the Lexington Pike in Garrard County, and was owned by B.M. Jones. She gives the date of her birth as April 14, 1847. Aunt Harriet's father was Daniel Scott, a slave out of Mote Scott's slave family. Aunt Harriet's mother's name was Amy Jones, slave of Marse Briar Jones, who came from Harrodsburg, Ky. The names of her brothers were Harrison, Daniel, Merida, and Ned; her sisters were Susie and Maria. Miss Patsy, wife of Marse Briar gave Maria to Marse Sammy Welsh, brother of Miss Patsy's and who lived with his sister. He taught school in Bryantsville for a long time. "General Gano who married Jane Welsh, adopted daughter of Marse Briar Jones, took my sisters Myra and Emma, Brother Ned and myself to Tarrant County, Texas to a town called Lick Skillet, to live. Grapevine was the name of the white folks house. It was called Grapevine because these grapevines twined around the house and arbors. Sister Emma was the cook and Myra and me were nurse and house maids. Brother married Betty Estill, a slave who cooked for the Estill family. Mr. Estill later bought Ned in order to keep him on the place. I didn't sleep in the cabins with the rest of the Negroes; I slept in the big house and nursed the children. I was not paid any money for my work. My food was the same as what the white folks et. In the summer time we wore cotton and tow linen; and linsey in the winter. The white folks took me to church and dressed me well. I had good shoes and they took me to church on Sunday. My master was a preacher and a doctor and a fine man. Miss Mat sho was hard to beat. The house they lived in was a big white house with two long porches. We had no overseer or driver. We had no "Po white neighbors". There was about 300 acres of land around Lick Skillet, but we did not have many slaves. The slaves were waked up by General Gano who rang a big farm bell about four times in the morning. There was no jail on the place and I never say a slave whipped or punished in any way. I never saw a slave auctioned off. My Mistus taught all the slaves to read and write, and we set on a bench in the dining room. When the news came that we were free General Gano took us all in the dining room and told us about it. I told him I wusn't going to the cabins and sleep with them niggers and I didn't. At Christmas and New Years we sho did have big times and General Gano and Miss Nat would buy us candy, popcorn, and firecrackers and all the good things just like the white folks. I don't remember any weddings, but do remember the funeral of Mr. Marion who lived between the big house and Lick Skillet. He was going to be buried in the cemetery at Lick Skillet, but the horses got scared and turned the spring wagon over and the corpse fell out. The mourners sure had a time getting things straightened out, but they finally got him buried.

They used to keep watermelon to pass to company. Us children would go to the patch and bring the melons to the big spring and pour water over them and cool 'em. When news came that we were free we all started back to Kentucky to Marse Jones old place. We started the journey in two covered wagons and an ambulance. General Gano and Miss Nat and the two children and me rode in the ambulance. When we got to Memphis we got on a steam boat named "Old Kentucky". We loaded the ambulance and the two wagons and horses on the boat. When we left the boat, we got on the train and got off at Georgetown in Scott County and rode from there to General Gano's Brother William in Scott County, on a stage coach. When I took the children, Katy and Maurice, upstairs to wash them I looked out the window into the driveway and saw the horses that belonged to Marse Briar Jones. They nickered at the gate trying to get in. The horses were named Henry Clay and Dan. When the children went down I waved at the horses and they looked up at the window and nickered again and seemed to know me. When we were coming back from Texas, Maurice held on the plait of my hair all the way back. I didn't marry while I belonged to the Gano family. I married Henry Mason after I came to Lancaster to live about sixty years ago. I am the mother of nine children, three boys and six girls. There are two living. I have no grand-children. I joined the church when the cholera epidemic broke out in Lancaster in 1878. The preacher was Brother Silas Crawford, of the Methodist Church. I was baptized in a pond on Creamery Street. I think people ought to be religious because they live better and they love people more."

Aunt Harriet lived at the present behind the White Methodist Church in Lancaster. The daughter with whom she lives is considered one of the high class of colored people in Lancaster. She holds an A.B. Degree, teaching in the colored city school, and is also a music teacher. She stands by the teaching of her mother, being a "Good Methodist"; giving of her time, talent, and service for her church.

Bibliography:
Interview with Aunt Harriet Mason, Lancaster, Kentucky.

15. GARRARD COUNTY. KENTUCKY EX-SLAVE STORIES.
(Eliza Ison)

SUBJECT INTERVIEWED: AUNT BELLE ROBINSON:

I found Aunt Belle sitting on the porch, dressed nice and clean with a white handkerchief pinned on her neck. When I went to her and told her who I was and the reason for my visit her face beamed with smiles and she said "Lawdy, it has been so long that I have forgot nearly everything I knew".

Further investigation soon proved that she had not forgotten, for her statements were very intelligent. She was working on a quilt and close investigation found that the work was well done. Aunt Belle tells me "I was born June 3rd, 1853 in Garrard County near Lancaster. My mother's name was Marion Blevin and she belonged to the family of Pleas Blevin. My father's name was Arch Robinson who lived in Madison County. Harrison Brady bought me from Ole Miss Nancy Graham and when Mr. Brady died and his property was sold Mrs. Brady bought me back; and she always said that she paid $400 for me. I lived in that family for three generations, until every one of them died. I was the only child and had always lived at the big house with my mistus. I wore the same kind of clothes and ate the same kind of food the white people ate. My mother and father lived at the cabin in the yard and my mother did the cooking for the family. My father did the work on the farm with the help that was hired from the neighbors. I was too young to remember much about the slave days, but I never heard of any slaves of the neighbors being punished. My "Mistus" always took me to the Baptist Church with her. I do not remember any preacher's names or any songs they sang."

Bibliography:
Interview with Aunt Belle Robinson, Ex-Slave of Garrard County.

16. INTERVIEWER: MRS. ZILLAH CROSS PEEL
PERSON INTERVIEWED: "AUNT ADELINE"   AGE: 89
HOME: 101 ROCK STREET, FAYETTEVILLE, ARKANSAS

"I was born a slave about 1848, in Hickmon County, Tennessee," said Aunt Adeline who lives as care taker in a house at 101 Rock Street, Fayetteville, Arkansas, which is owned by the Blakely-Hudgens estate.

Aunt Adeline has been a slave and a servant in five generations of the Parks family. Her mother, Liza, with a group of five Negroes, was sold into slavery to John P.A. Parks, in Tennessee, about 1840.

"When my mother's master come to Arkansas about 1849, looking for a country residence, he bought what was known as the old Kidd place on the Old Wire Road, which was one of the Stage Coach stops. I was about one year old when we came. We had a big house and many times passengers would stay several days and wait for the next stage to come by. It was then that I earned my first money. I must have been about six or seven years old. One of Mr. Parks' daughters was about one and a half years older than I was. We had a play house back of the fireplace chimney. We didn't have many toys; maybe a doll made of a corn cob, with a dress made from scraps and a head made from a roll of scraps. We were playing church. Miss Fannie was the preacher and I was the audience. We were singing "Jesus my all to Heaven is gone." When we were half way through with our song we discovered that the passengers from the stage coach had stopped to listen. We were so frightened at our audience that we both ran. But we were coaxed to come back for a dime and sing our song over. I remember that Miss Fannie used a big leaf for a book.

"I had always been told from the time I was a small child that I was a Negro of African stock. That it was no disgrace to be a Negro and had it not been for the white folks who brought us over here from Africa as slaves, we would never have been here and would have been much better off.

"We colored folks were not allowed to be taught to read or write. It was against the law. My master's folks always treated me well. I had good clothes. Sometimes I was whipped for things I should not have done just as the white children were.

"When a young girl was married her parents would always give her a slave. I was given by my master to his daughter, Miss Elizabeth, who married Mr. Blakely. I was just five years old. She moved into a new home at Fayetteville and I was taken along but she soon sent me back home to my master telling him that I was too little and not enough help to her. So I went back to the Parks home and stayed until I was over seven years old. [1]My master made a bill of sale for me to his daughter, in order to keep account of all settlements, so when he died and the estate settled each child would know how he stood.

"I was about 15 years old when the Civil War ended and was still living with Mrs. Blakely and helped care for her little children. Her daughter, Miss Lenora, later married H.M. Hudgens, and I then went to live with her and cared for her children. When her daughter Miss Helen married Professor Wiggins, I took care of her little daughter, and this made five generations that I have cared for.

"During the Civil War, Mr. Parks took all his slaves and all of his fine stock, horses and cattle and went South to Louisiana following the Southern army for protection. Many slave owners left the county taking with them their slaves and followed the army.

"When the war was over, Mr. Parks was still in the South and gave to each one of his slaves who did not want to come back to Arkansas so much money. My uncle George came back with Mr. Parks and was given a good mountain farm of forty acres, which he put in cultivation and one of my uncle's descendants still lives on the place. My mother did not return to Arkansas but went on to Joplin, Missouri, and for more than fifty years, neither one of us knew where the other one was until one day a man from Fayetteville went into a restaurant in Joplin and ordered his breakfast, and my mother who was in there heard him say he lived in Fayetteville, Arkansas. He lived just below the Hudgens home and when my mother enquired about the family he told her I was still alive and was with the family. While neither of us could read nor write we corresponded through different people. But I never saw her after I was eleven years old. Later Mr. Hudgens went to Joplin to see if she was well taken care of. She owned her own little place and when she died there was enough money for her to be buried.

"Civil War days are vivid to me. The Courthouse which was then in the middle of the Square was burned one night by a crazy Confederate soldier. The old men in the town saved him and then put him in the county jail to keep him from burning other houses. Each family was to take food to him and they furnished bedding. The morning I was to take his breakfast, he had ripped open his feather bed and crawled inside to get warm. The room was so full of feathers when I got there that his food nearly choked him. I had carried him ham, hot biscuits and a pot of coffee.

"After the War many soldiers came to my mistress, Mrs. Blakely, trying to make her free me. I told them I was free but I did not want to go anywhere, that I wanted to stay in the only home that I had ever known. In a way that placed me in a wrong attitude. I was pointed out as different. Sometimes I was threatened for not leaving but I stayed on.

"I had always been well treated by my master's folks. While we lived at the old Kidd place, there was a church a few miles from our home. My uncle George was coachman and drove my master's family in great splendor in a fine barouche to church. After the war, when he went to his own place, Mr. Parks gave him the old carriage and bought a new one for the family.

"I can remember the days of slavery as happy ones. We always had an abundance of food. Old Aunt Martha cooked and there was always plenty prepared for all the white folks as well as the colored folks. There was a long table at the end of the big kitchen for the colored folks. The vegetables were all prepared of an evening by Aunt Martha with someone to help her.

"My mother seemed to have a gift of telling fortunes. She had a brass ring about the size of a dollar with a handwoven knotted string that she used.

I remember that she told many of the young people in the neighborhood many strange things. They would come to her with their premonitions.

"Yes, we were afraid of the patyroles. All colored folks were. They said that any Negroes that were caught away from their master's premises without a permit would be whipped by the patyroles. They used to sing a song:

'Run nigger run,
The patyroles
Will get you.'

"Yes'm, the War separated lots of families. Mr. Parks' son, John C. Parks, enlisted in Colonel W.H. Brooks' regiment at Fayetteville as third lieutenant. Mr. Jim Parks was killed at the Battle of Getysburg.

"I do remember it was my mistress, Mrs. Blakely, who kept the Masonic Building from being burned. The soldiers came to set it on fire. Mrs. Blakely knew that if it burned, our home would burn as it was just across the street. Mrs. Blakely had two small children who were very ill in upstairs rooms. She told the soldiers if they burned the Masonic Building that her house would burn and she would be unable to save her little children. They went away."

While Aunt Adeline is nearing ninety, she is still active, goes shopping and also tends to the many crepe myrtle bushes as well as many other flowers at the Hudgens place.

She attends to the renting of the apartment house, as caretaker, and is taken care of by members of the Blakely-Hudgens families.

Aunt Adeline talks "white folks language," as they say, and seldom associates with the colored people of the town.

[1]   This statement can be verified by the will made by John P.A. Parks, and filed in Probate Court in the clerk's office in Washington County.

17. INTERVIEW OF MISS MARY JANE WILSON
Portsmouth, Virginia By—Thelma Dunston

NEGRO PIONEER TEACHER OF PORTSMOUTH, VIRGINIA

One of the rooms in the Old Folks Home for Colored in Portsmouth, Virginia is occupied by an ex-slave—one of the first Negro teachers of Portsmouth.

On meeting Miss Mary Jane Wilson, very little questioning was needed to get her to tell of her life. Drawing her chair near a small stove, she said, "my Mother and Father was slaves, and when I was born, that made me a slave. I was the only child. My Mother was owned by one family, and my Father was owned by another family. My mother and father was allowed to live together. One day my father's mastah took my father to Norfolk and put him in a jail to stay until he could sell him. My missus bought my father so he could be with us."

"During this time I was small, and I didn't have so much work to do. I jus helped around the house."

"I was in the yard one day, and I saw so many men come marching down the street, I ran and told my mother what I'd seen. She tried to tell me what it was all about, but I couldn't understand her. Not long after that we was free."

Taking a long breath, the old woman said, "My father went to work in the Norfolk Navy Yard as a teamster. He began right away buying us a home. We was one of the first Negro land owners in Portsmouth after emancipation. My father builded his own house. It's only two blocks from here, and it still stands with few improvements."

With a broad smile Miss Wilson added, "I didn't get any teachings when I was a slave. When I was free, I went to school. The first school I went to was held in a church. Soon they builded a school building that was called, 'Chestnut Street Academy', and I went there. After finishing Chestnut Street Academy, I went to Hampton Institute. In 1874, six years after Hampton Institute was started, I graduated."

At this point Miss Wilson's pride was unconcealed. She continued her conversation, but her voice was much louder and her speech was much faster. She remarked, "My desire was to teach. I opened a school in my home, and I had lots of students. After two years my class grew so fast and large that my father built a school for me in our back yard. I had as many as seventy-five pupils at one time. Many of them became teachers. I had my graduation exercises in the Emanuel A. M. E. Church. Those were my happiest days."

18. FLORIDA FOLKLORE

Jules Abner Frost
May 19, 1937

"MAMA DUCK"

1. Name and address of informant, **MAMA DUCK**, Governor & India Sts., Tampa, Florida.

2. Date and time of interview, May 19, 1937, 9:30 A.M.

3. Place of interview, her home, above address.

4. Name and address of person, if any, who put you in touch with informant, J.D. Davis (elevator operator), 1623 Jefferson St., Tampa, Florida.

5. Name and address of person, if any accompanying you (none).

6. Description of room, house, surroundings, etc.

Two-room unpainted shack, leaky roof, most window panes missing, porch dangerous to walk on. House standing high on concrete blocks. Located in alley, behind other Negro shacks.

NOTE: Letter of Feb. 17, 1939, from Mr. B.A. Botkin to Dr. Corse states that my ex-slave story, "Mama Duck" is marred by use of the question and answer method. In order to make this material of use as American Folk Stuff material, I have rewritten it, using the first person, as related by the informant.

Personal History of Informant

[TR: Repetitive information removed.]

1. Ancestry: Negro.

2. Place and date of birth: Richard (probably Richmond), Va., about 1828.

3. Family: unknown.

4. Places lived in, with dates: Has lived in Tampa since about 1870.

5. Education, with dates: Illiterate.

6. Occupations and accomplishments, with dates: None. Informant was a slave, and has always performed common labor.

7. Special skills and interests: none.

8. Community and religious activities: none.

9. Description of informant: Small, emaciated, slightly graying, very thin kinky hair, tightly braided in small pigtails. Somewhat wrinkled, toothless. Active for her age, does washing for a living.

10. Other points gained in interview: Strange inability of local Old Age Pension officials to establish right of claimants to benefits. Inexplainable causes of refusal of direct relief.

MAMA DUCK

Gwan away f'm here, Po'-Boy; dat gemmen ain't gwine feed you nuthin. You keep yo' dirty paws offen his close.

Come in, suh. Take care you don't fall thoo dat ol' po'ch flo'; hit 'bout ready to go t' pieces, but I 'way behind on rent, so I cain't ask 'em to have hit fixed. Dis ol' house aint fitten fer nobody t' live in; winder glass gone an' roof leaks. Young folks in dese parts done be'n usin' it fer a co't house 'fore I come; you know—a place to do dey courtin' in. Kep' a-comin' atter I done move in, an' I had to shoo 'em away.

Dat young rascal comin' yondah, he one of 'em. I claiah to goodness, I wisht I had a fence to keep folks outa my yahd. Reckon you don't know what he be quackin' lak dat fer. Dat's 'cause my name's "Mama Duck." He doin' it jus' t' pester me. But dat don't worry me none; I done quit worryin'.

I sho' had plenty chance to worry, though. Relief folks got me on dey black list. Dey give rashuns to young folks what's wukkin' an' don't give me nary a mouthful. Reason fer dat be 'cause dey wanted me t' go t' de porehouse. I wanted t' take my trunk 'long, an' dey wouldn't lemme. I got some things in dere I be'n havin' nigh onto a hunnert years. Got my ol' blue-back Webster, onliest book I evah had, 'scusin' mah Bible. Think I wanna th'ow dat away? No-o suh!

So dey black-list me, 'cause I won't kiss dey feets. I ain't kissin nobody's, wouldn't kiss my own mammy's.

I nevah see my mammy. She put me in a hick'ry basket when I on'y a day and a half old, with nuthin' on but mah belly band an' di'per. Took me down in de cotton patch an' sot de basket on a stump in de bilin sun. Didn't want me, 'cause I be black. All de otha youngins o' hers be bright.

Gran'mammy done tol' me, many a time, how she heah me bawlin' an' go an' git me, an' fotch me to mammy's house; but my own mammy, she say, tu'n me down cold.

"Dat you, Mammy" she say, sweet as pie, when gran'mammy knock on de do'.

"Dont you nevah call me 'Mammy' no mo'," gran'mammy tol' 'er. "Any woman what'd leave a po' li'l mite lak dat to perish to death ain't fitten t' be no dotter o' mine."

So gran'mammy tuk me to raise, an' I ain't nevah wanted no mammy but her. Nevah knowed who my daddy was, an' I reckon my mammy didn't know, neithah. I bawn at Richard, Vahjinny. My sistah an' brothah be'n dead too many years to count; I de las' o' de fam'ly.

I kin remember 'fore de fust war start. I had three chillen, boys, taller'n me when freedom come. Mah fust mastah didn't make de li'l chillen wuk none. All I done was play. W'en I be ol' enough t' wuk, dey tuk us to Pelman, Jawjah. I never wukked in de fiel's none, not den. Dey allus le me nuss de chillens.

Den I got married. Hit wa'nt no church weddin'; we got married in gran'mammy's kitchen, den we go to our own log house. By an' by mah mahster sol' me an' mah baby to de man what had de plantation nex' to ours. His name was John Lee. He was good to me, an' let me see my chillens.

I nevah got no beatin's. Onliest thing I evah got was a li'l slap on de han', lak dat. Didn't hurt none. But I'se seen cullud men on de Bradley plantation git tur'ble beatin's. De whippin' boss was Joe Sylvester, a white man. He had pets mongst de wimmen folks, an' used t' let 'em off easy, w'en dey desarved a good beatin'. Sometimes 'e jes' bop 'em crost de ear wid a battlin' stick, or kick 'em in de beehind.

You don't know what's a battlin' stick? Well, dis here be one. You use it fer washin' close. You lif's de close outa de wash pot wid dis here battlin' stick; den you tote 'em to de battlin' block—dis here stump. Den you beat de dirt out wid de battlin' stick.

De whippin' boss got pets 'mongst de mens, too, but dey got it a li'l wusser'n de wimmens. Effen dey wan't too mean, he jes' strap 'em 'crost de sharp side of a bar'l an' give 'em a few right smaht licks wid a bull whip.

But dey be some niggahs he whip good an' hard. If dey sass back, er try t' run away, he mek 'em cross dey han's lak dis; den he pull 'em up, so dey toes jes' tetch de ground'; den he smack 'em crost de back an' rump wid a big wood paddle, fixed full o' holes. Know what dem holes be for? Ev'y hole mek a blister. Den he mek 'em lay down on de groun', whilst he bus' all dem blisters wid a rawhide whip.

I nevah heard o' nobody dyin' f'm gittin' a beatin'. Some couldn't wuk fer a day or so. Sometimes de whippin' boss th'ow salt brine on dey backs, or smear on turpentine, to mek it well quicker.

I don't know, 'zackly, how old I is. Mebbe—wait a minute, I didn't show you my pitcher what was in de paper. I cain't read, but somebody say dey put down how old I is undah mah pitcher. Dar hit—don't dat say a hunndrt an' nine? I reckon dat be right, seein' I had three growed-up boys when freedom come.

Dey be on'y one sto' here when I come to Tampa. Hit b'long t' ol' man Mugge. Dey be a big cotton patch where Plant City is now. I picked some cotton dere, den I come to Tampa, an' atter a while I got a job nussin' Mister Perry Wall's chillen. Cullud folks jes' mek out de bes' dey could. Some of 'em lived in tents, till dey c'd cut logs an' build houses wid stick-an'-dirt chimbleys.

Lotta folks ask me how I come to be called "Mama Duck." Dat be jes' a devil-ment o' mine. I named my own se'f dat. One day when I be 'bout twelve year old, I come home an' say, "Well, gran'mammy, here come yo' li'l ducky home again." She hug me an' say, "Bress mah li'l ducky." Den she keep on callin' me dat, an' when I growed up, folks jes' put de "Mama" on.

I reckon I a heap bettah off dem days as I is now. Allus had sumpin t' eat an' a place t' stay. No sech thing ez gittin' on a black list dem days. Mighty hard on a pusson ol' az me not t' git no rashuns an' not have no reg'lar job.

19. GARRARD CO. KENTUCKY
(Sue Higgins)

STORY OF AUNT HARRIET MASON AGE 100—A SLAVE GIRL:

"When I was seven years old my missis took me to Bourbon County, when we got to Lexington I tried to run off and go back to Bryantsville to see my mammy. Mas'r Gano told me if I didn't come the sheriff would git me. I never liked to go to Lexington since.

"One Sunday we was going to a big meetin' we heared som'in rattling in the weeds. It was a big snake, it made a track in the dust. When we got home missis asked me if I killed any snakes. I said to missis, snake like to got me and Gilbert, too.

"They used to have dances at Mrs. Dickerson's, a neighbor of General Gano (a preacher in the Christian Church). Mrs. Dickerson wouldn't let the "Padaroes" come to the dances. If they did come, whe[TR:she?] would get her pistol and make them leave.

"When General Gano went from Texas to Kentucky, he brought 650 head of horses. He sold all of them but Old Black.

"Mas'r Gano went back to Texas to take up a child he had buried there. The boat blowed up, and he came nigh gittin' drowned.

"One time I wus out in Mas'rs wheat field. I would get the wheat heads and make chewin' wax. I told missis I want to go up to Bryantsville to see my mammy. Mas'r took me in about a week.

"Up at Miss Jennie West's house they had an ole icehouse. Some boys made out like they had a bear up there to scare every body away.

"I saw a flock of wild geese fly over one evenin' late. Some boys saw them and one boy shot the leader. The rest of the flock wound round and round, they didn't know where to go.

"One time when I was actin' nurse for missis, there was another nigger gal there and we was playin' horse-shoes. Celia hit me in the head. It got blood all over the baby's dress. Missis came out, she say, "I'll hit you niggers if you don't stop playing with horse-shoes." The scar is on my head yet whar Celia hit me. I ain't played since. Do you blame me?

"Missis told her brother Sam one day to whoop me. Every time he hit me, I'd hit him. I wan't feared then. I didn't know no better. Look like white folks goin' to have their way and niggers goin' to have theirs.

"I used to say I wish I'd died when I was little. But now I thank De Lord I'm here and I want to stay here as long as Lilly (my daughter) lives.

"Missis wanted all of us little niggers to call Kate, Missis' little daughter, Miss Kate. But missis say, "They will call me old missis then".

"Kate had red hair. A little nigger boy say, 'Look! Harriet, the town's on fire', I say git away from here nigger, I ain't goin' to have you makin' fun of my chil'en.

"Me and missis was goin' to a neighbor's house one day in a sleigh. The baby was wrapped up in a comfort (it had a hole in it). The baby slipped out. I say, 'Lor' missis, you're lost that baby.'

"No, I haven't, Missis say. We stopped and shook the comfort and John was gone. 'Ain't that awful, Miss Mat?' We went back and found him a mile behind."

I asked Aunt Harriet to sing. She said, "I have to wait for the speret to move me". (S. Higgins).

20. INTERVIEWER: MISS IRENE ROBERTSON
PERSON INTERVIEWED: LIDDIE AIKEN, WHEATLEY, ARKANSAS
AGE: 62

"My mother was born in southwest Georgia close to the Alabama line. Her mother come from Virginia. She was sold with her mother and two little brothers. Her mother had been sold and come in a wagon to southwest Georgia. They was all field hands. They cleaned out new ground. They was afraid of hoop-snakes. She said they look like a hoop rolling and whatever they stuck a horn or their tail in it died. They killed trees.

"Mama said she druther plough than chop. She was a big woman and they let her plough right along by her two little brothers, Henry and Will Keller. Will et so many sweet potatoes they called him 'Tater Keller.' After he got grown we come out here. Folks called him 'Tate Keller.' Henry died. I recollect Uncle Tate.

"I was born close to Mobile, Alabama. Mama was named Sarah Keller. Grandma was called Mariah. Banks Tillman sold her the first time. Bill Keller bought them all the last time. His wife was named Ada Keller. They had a great big family but I forgot what they said about them. Mack clem up in a persimmon tree one day and the old man hollered at him, 'Get out of that tree 'fore you fall.' 'Bout then the boy turned 'loose and fell. It knocked the breath out him. It didn't kill him. Three or four of Miss Ada's children died with congestive chills. Mama said the reason they had them chills they played down at the gin pond all the time. It was shady and a pretty place and they was allowed to play in the pond. Three or four of them died nearly in a heap.

"One of the boys had a pet billy-goat. It got up on top mama's house one time. It would bleat and look down at them. They was afraid it would jump down on them if they went out. It chewed up things Aunt Beanie washed. She had them put out on bushes and might had a line too. They fattened it and killed it. Mama said Mr. Bill Keller never had nothing too good to divide with his niggers. I reckon by that they got some of the goat.

"They lived like we live now. Every family done his own cooking. I don't know how many families lived on the place.

"I know about the Yankees. They come by and every one of the men and boys went with them but Uncle Cal. He was cripple and they advised him not to start. Didn't none of the women go. Mama said she never seen but one ever come back. She thought they got killed or went on some place else.

"Mr. Keller died and Miss Ada went back to her folks. They left everything in our care that they didn't move. She took all her house things. They sold or took all their stock. They left us a few cows and pigs. I don't know how long they stayed after the old man died. His children was young; he might not been so old.

"I recollect grandma. She smoked a pipe nearly all the time. My papa was a livery stable man. He was a fine man with stock. He was a little black man. Mama was too big. Grandma was taller but she was slick black. He lived at Mobile, Alabama. I was the onliest child mama had. Uncle 'Tate Keller' took grandma and mama to Mobile. He never went to the War. He was a good carpenter and he worked out when he didn't have a lot to do in the field. He was off at work when all the black men and boys left Mr. Bill. He never went back after they left till freedom.

"They didn't know when freedom took place. They was all scattering for two years about to get work and something to eat. Tate come and got them. They went off in a wagon that Tate made for his master, Bill Keller. We come to Tupelo, Mississippi from Mobile when I was a little bit of a girl. Then we made one crop and come to Helena. Uncle Tate died there and mama died at Crocketts Bluff. My papa died back in Mobile, Alabama. He was breaking a young horse and got throwed up side a tree. He didn't live long then.

"I got three boys now and I had seben—all boys. They farms and do public work. Tom is in Memphis. Pete is in Helena and I live wid Macon between here (Wheatley) and Cotton Plant. We farm. I done everything could be thought of on a farm. I ploughed some less than five year ago. I liked to plough. My boy ploughs all he can now and we do the chopping. We all pick cotton and get in the corn. We work day laborers now.

"If I was young the times wouldn't stand in my way. I could make it. I don't know what is the trouble lessen some wants too much. They can't get it. We has a living and thankful for it. I never 'plied for no help yet.

"I still knits my winter stockings. I got knitting needles and cards my own mother had and used. I got use for them. I wears clothes on my body in cold weather. One reason you young folks ain't no 'count you don't wear enough clothes when it is cold. I wear flannel clothes if I can get holt of them.

"Education done ruint the world. I learnt to read a little. I never went to school. I learnt to work. I learnt my boys to go with me to the field and not to be ashamed to sweat. It's healthy. They all works."

21. INTERVIEWER: MISS IRENE ROBERTSON
PERSON INTERVIEWED: MATTIE ALDRIDGE
HAZEN, ARKANSAS
AGE: 60?

"My mother's old owner named Master Sanders. She born somewhere in Tennessee. I heard her say she lived in Mississippi. I was born in Tennessee. My pa was born in Mississippi. I know he belong to the Duncans. His name George Washington Duncan. There ain't nary drap white blood in none us. I got four brothers. I do remembers grandma. She set and tell us tales bout old times like you want to know. Been so long I forgotten. Ma was a house girl and pa a field hand. Way grandma talked it must of been hard to find out what white folks wanted em to do, cause she couldn't tell what you say some times. She never did talk plain.

"They was glad when freedom declared. They said they was hard on em. Whoop em. Pa was killed in Crittenden County in Arkansas. He was clearin' new ground. A storm come up and a limb hit him. It killed him. Grandma and ma allus say like if you build a house you want to put all the winders in you ever goin' to want. It bad luck to cut in and put in nother one. Sign of a death. I ain't got no business tellin' you bout that. White folks don't believe in signs.

"I been raisin' up childern—'dopted childern, washin', ironin', scourin', hoein', gatherin' corn, pickin' cotton, patchin', cookin'. They ain't nothin' what I ain't done.

"No'm, I sure ain't voted. I don't believe in women votin'. They don't know who to vote for. The men don't know neither. If folks visited they would care more bout the other an wouldn't be so much devilment goin' on."

22. VIRGINIA NEWMAN, BEAUMONT, TEXAS.

Virginia Newman was freeborn, the daughter of a Negro boat captain and a part Negro, part Indian mother. When a young girl, Virginia apprenticed herself, and says she was nursegirl in the family of Gov. Foster, of Louisiana. She does not know her age, but says she saw the "Stars fall" in 1833. She has the appearance of extreme old age, and is generally conceded to be 100 years old or more. She now lives in Beaumont, Texas.

"When de stars fall I's 'bout six year old. They didn' fall on de grou'. They cross de sky like a millions of firebugs.

"My fus' name Georgia Turner, 'cause my pappy's name George Turner, and he a freeborn nigger man. He's captain of a boat, but they call 'em vessels them days. It have livin' quarters in it and go back and forth 'tween dis place and dat and go back to Africy, too.

"My grandmudder, she an Africy woman. They brung her freeborn from Africy and some people what knowed things one time tol' us we too proud but us had reason to be proud. My grandmudder's fambly in Africy was a African prince of de rulin' people. My udder grandmudder was a pure bred Indian woman and she raise all my mudder's chillen. My mudder name Eli Chivers.

"When I's small I live with my grandmudder in a old log cabin on the ribber, 'way out in de bresh jus' like de udder Indians live. I's born on my fadder's big boat, 'way below Grades Island, close by Franklin, in Louisiana. They tells me he carry cargo of cotton in de hull of de boat, and when I's still li'l they puts out to sea, and grandmudder, Sarah Turner her name, tuk us and kep' us with her in de cabin.

"Us didn' have stick of furniture in de house, no bed, no chair, no nothin'. Us cut saplings boughs for bed, with green moss over 'em. Us was happy, though. Us climb trees and play. It was hard sometime to git things to eat so far in de woods and us eat mos' everything what run or crawl or fly outdoors. Us eat many rattlesnake and them's fine eatin'. We shoot de snake and skin him and cut him in li'l dices. Den us stew him slow with lots of brown gravy.

"They allus askin' me now make hoe-cake like we et. Jus' take de cornmeal and salt and water and make patties with de hands and wrop de sof' patties in cabbage leafs, stir out de ashes and put de patties in de hot ashes. Dat was good.

"One my grandfadders a old Mexican man call Old Man Caesar. All de grandfolks was freeborn and raise de chillen de same, but when us gits big they tell us do what we wants. Us could stay in de woods and be free or go up to live with de white folks. I's a purty big gal when I goes up to de big house and 'prentice myself to work for de Fosters. Dey have big plantation at Franklin and lots of slaves. One time de Governor cripple in de leg and I do nothin' but nuss him.

"I's been so long in de woods and don' see nobody much dat I love it up with de white folks. Dey 'lowed us have dances and when dat old 'cordian starts to play, iffen I ain't git my hair comb yit, it don't git comb. De boss man like to see de niggers 'joy demselves. Us dance de quadrille.

"Us have 'ceptional marsters. My fadder sick on Marster Lewis' plantation and can't walk and de marster brung him a 'spensive reclinin' chair. Old Judge Lewis was his marster.

"I git marry from de plantation and my husban' he name Beverly Newman and hc from de Lewis plantation in Opelousas. They read out'n de Book and after de readin' us have lots of white folks to come and watch us have big dance.

"When a nigger do wrong den, they didn' send him to de pen. They put him 'cross a barrel and strop him behin'.

"When fightin' 'gin, all our white folks and us slaves have to go 'way from Louisiana. Opelousas and them place was free long time 'fore de udders. Us strike out for Texas and it took mos' a year to walk from de Bayou la Fouche to de Brazos bottoms. I have to tote my two li'l boys, dat was Jonah and Simon. They couldn' neither walk yit. Us have de luggage in de ox cart and us have to walk. Dey was some mo' cullud people and white and de mud drag de feetses and stick up de wheels so dey couldn' even move. Us all walk barefeets and our feets break and run they so sore, and blister for months. It cold and hot sometime and rain and us got no house or no tent.

"De white folks settles in Jasper county, on a plantation dere. After while freedom come to Texas, too, but mos' de slaves stay round de old marsters. I's de only one what go back to Louisiana. After de war my fambly git broke up and my three oldes' chillen never see de li'l ones. Dose later chillen, dey's eight livin' now out'n nine what was born since slavery and my fourth chile die seven year ago when she 75 year old.

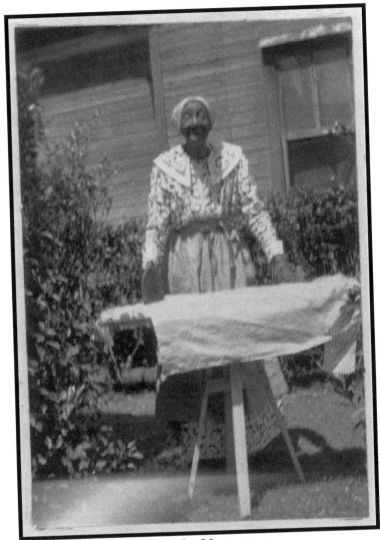

Virginia Newman

"When I git back to Louisiana I come to be a midwife and I brung so many babies here I can't count. De old priest say I ought to have a big book with all their names to 'member by.

"It were 'bout dis time I have my fur' bought dress and it was blue guinea with yaller spots. It were long at de ankle and make with a body wais'. Us wore lots of unnerwear and I ain't take 'em off yit.

99

"I never been sick, I's jus' weak. I almos' go blin' some time back but now I git my secon' sight and I sees well 'nough to sew."

Slavery Books & African American History Courses & Resources
https://africanamericanhistorybooks.blogspot.com

WWW.HISTORICPUBLISHING.COM

Made in the USA
Middletown, DE
22 August 2024